VOWEL SOUNDS

Symbol	Examples
a	**a**ct, b**a**t
ā	d**ay**, **a**ge
âr	**air**, d**are**
ä	f**a**ther, st**ar**
e	**e**dge, t**e**n
ē	sp**ee**d, mon**ey**
ə*	**a**go, syst**e**m, easi**l**y, c**o**mpete, foc**u**s
ēr	d**ear**, p**ier**
i	f**i**t, **i**s
ī	sk**y**, b**i**te
o	n**o**t, w**a**sp
ō	n**o**se, **o**ver
ô	l**aw**, **o**rder
oi	n**oi**se, enj**oy**
o͞o	tr**u**e, b**oo**t
oo	p**u**t, l**oo**k
yo͞o	c**u**te, **u**nited
ou	l**ou**d, c**ow**
u	f**u**n, **u**p
ûr	l**ear**n, **ur**ge, butt**er**, w**or**d

*This symbol, the *schwa*, represents the sound of unaccented vowels. It sounds like "uh."

CONSONANT SOUNDS

Symbol	Examples
b	**b**ack, ca**b**
ch	**ch**eap, ma**tch**, pi**c**ture
d	**d**oor, hea**d**
f	**f**an, lea**f**, **ph**one
g	**g**ive, do**g**
h	**h**er, be**h**ave
j	**j**ust, pa**g**e
k	**k**ing, ba**k**e, **c**ar
l	**l**eaf, ro**ll**
m	**m**y, ho**m**e
n	**n**ote, rai**n**
ng	si**ng**, ba**n**k
p	**p**ut, sto**p**
r	**r**ed, fa**r**
s	**s**ay, pa**ss**
sh	**sh**ip, pu**sh**
t	**t**o, le**t**
th	**th**in, wi**th**
TH	**TH**at, ba**TH**e
v	**v**alue, li**v**e
w	**w**ant, a**w**ay
y	**y**es, on**i**on
z	**z**oo, ma**z**e, ri**s**e
zh	plea**s**ure, vi**s**ion

INTERACTIVE VOCABULARY

INTERACTIVE VOCABULARY

General Words

Third Edition

Amy E. Olsen
Cuesta College

New York   San Francisco   Boston
London   Toronto   Sydney   Tokyo   Singapore   Madrid
Mexico City   Munich   Paris   Cape Town   Hong Kong   Montreal

Acquisitions Editor: Melanie Craig
Associate Editor: Frederick Speers
Marketing Manager: Thomas DeMarco
Senior Supplements Editor: Donna Campion
Media Supplements Editor: Jenna Egan
Production Manager: Donna DeBenedictis
Project Coordination, Text Design, and Electronic Page Makeup: Elm Street Publishing Services, Inc.
Cover Designer/Manager: Wendy Ann Fredericks
Cover Photos: Clockwise from top left: Stuart Westmorland/Getty; Popperfoto/Alamy; Peter/Georgina Bowater/Mira; and AP/Wideworld.
Art Studio: Elm Street Publishing Services, Inc.; Gil Adams
Photo Researcher: Chrissy McIntyre
Manufacturing Buyer: Roy L. Pickering, Jr.
Printer and Binder: R. R. Donnelley & Sons Company/Willard
Cover Printer: Coral Graphic Services, Inc.

Photo Credits: P. 8 (top), Michael Newman/PhotoEdit; p. 8 (bottom), Stockbyte/Getty; p. 12, Michael Newman/PhotoEdit; p. 14, David Young-Wolff/Photo Edit; p. 20, Punchstock; p. 26, Felicia Martinez/PhotoEdit; p. 34, Getty Images; p. 38 (center left), Richard T. Nowitz/Corbis; p. 38 (top right), Keren Su/ Corbis; p. 38 (bottom right), Stuart Westmorland/Getty; p. 44 (top left), Ryan McVay/Getty; p. 44 (center right), Yann Arthus-Bertrand/Corbis; p. 44 (center left), Getty Images; p. 44 (bottom right), Stuart Westmorland/Getty; p. 50 (top), Popperfoto/Alamy; p. 50 (bottom), Laurence Dutton/Getty; p. 59, Erich Lessing/Art Resource, NY; p. 62, Bettmann/Corbis; p. 65, Stephen Oliver/DK; p. 68, Charbruken/Getty; p. 71, Siede Preis/Getty; p. 74 (left), Photofest NY; p. 74 (left), Milan Chuckovich/Stone/Getty; p. 78, Janie Christie/Getty; p. 82, Photodisc/Getty; p. 86 (top), Ariel Skelley/Corbis; p. 86 (right), Amwell/Getty; p. 92, Peter/Georgina Bowater/Mira; p. 95, Spike Mafford/PhotodiscGreen/Getty; p. 98, Michael Melford/NGS/Getty; p. 106, Connie Coleman/Getty; p. 110, Brand X Pictures/Alamy; p. 116, Arcaid/Alamy; p. 122, Bob Daemmrich Photo, Inc.; p. 124, Bill Aron/PhotoEdit; p. 130, John Lamb/Getty; p. 134, Werner Forman/Art Resource, NY; p. 137, Jeff Greenberg/Photo Edit; p. 143, Private Collection, Archives Charmet/Bridgeman Art Library; p. 146, Bettmann/Corbis; p. 152, AP/Wide World Photos; p. 154, AP/Wide World Photos; p. 160, C. Wilhelm/Photex/zefa/Corbis

Copyright © 2007 by Pearson Education, Inc.

All rights reserved. No part of this publication may be reproduced, stored in a retrieval system, or transmitted, in any form or by any means, electronic, mechanical, photocopying, recording, or otherwise, without the prior written permission of the publisher. Printed in the United States.

Please visit us at **www.ablongman.com/vocabulary**

ISBN 0-321-36497-X

1 2 3 4 5 6 7 8 9 10—DOW—09 08 07 06

DEDICATION

To my mom. Her smile, her warmth, and her enthusiasm were always inspiring and will always be so.

—*Amy E. Olsen*

CONTENTS

© 2007 Pearson Education, Inc.

PREFACE

Because students benefit greatly from increased word power, the study of vocabulary should be enjoyable. Unfortunately, vocabulary workbooks often lose sight of this goal. To help make the study of vocabulary an exciting and enjoyable part of college study, I wrote *Interactive Vocabulary*. The third edition of this book keeps the elements that make learning vocabulary enjoyable and adds new features in response to comments offered by instructors across the country who teach vocabulary and reading courses.

The goal of this book—the first level in a three-book interactive series—is to make the study of vocabulary fun through a variety of thematic readings, self-tests, and interactive exercises. As a casual glimpse through the book will indicate, these activities involve writing, personal experience, art, and many other formats. The goal of these activities is simple: to utilize individual learning styles to help students learn new words in a large number of contexts.

Underlying the text's strong visual appeal is a strong underlying philosophy: an essential part of learning vocabulary is repeated exposure to a word. *Interactive Vocabulary* provides nine exposures to each vocabulary word in the text plus more opportunities for exposure through the Collaborative Activities and games in the Instructor's Manual.

CONTENT OVERVIEW

Interactive Vocabulary is an ideal text for both classroom work and self-study. The twenty main chapters follow a specific and consistent format.

- **Thematic Reading**: Because most vocabulary is acquired through reading, each chapter, with the exception of the Word Parts and Review chapters, begins with a thematic reading that introduces ten vocabulary words in context. These readings come in a variety of formats including newspaper articles, journal entries, and interviews. The goal is to show that new words may be encountered anywhere. Rather than simply presenting a word list with definitions, the readings give students the opportunity to discover the meanings of these new words via context clues.

    The themes for *Interactive Vocabulary* were chosen from areas most interesting to students of all ages. In choosing the words, I was guided by five factors: (1) relation to the chapter theme, (2) use in popular magazines such as *Newsweek*, (3) listings in such frequency guides as *The American Heritage Word Frequency Book* and *The Educator's Word Frequency Guide*, (4) occurrence in standardized tests such as the SAT, and (5) my own experiences teaching developmental reading and writing.

- **Predicting**: A Predicting activity that gives students the chance to figure out the meaning of each vocabulary word before looking at the definition follows the thematic reading. The Predicting section helps students learn the value of context clues in determining the meaning of a word. While the text does offer information on dictionary use, I strongly advocate the use of context clues as one of the most active methods of vocabulary development.

- **Self-Tests**: Following the Predicting activity are four Self-Tests in various formats. With these tests, students can monitor their comprehension. The tests include text and sentence completion, true/false situations, matching, and analogies. Some tests employ context-clue strategies such as synonyms, antonyms, and general meaning. Critical thinking skills are an important part of each test. (Answers to the Self-Tests appear in the Instructor's Manual.)

© 2007 Pearson Education, Inc.

- **Interactive Exercise:** Following the Self-Tests is an Interactive Exercise that asks students to begin actively using the vocabulary words. The activity may include writing, answering questions, or making lists. The Interactive Exercises give students the chance to really think about the meanings of the words, and more importantly, they encourage students to begin using the words actively.
- **Hint:** Each chapter includes a hint for developing vocabulary, reading, or study skills. The hints are brief and practical, and students will be able to make use of them in all of their college courses.
- **Word List:** Following the Hint is a list of the vocabulary words with a pronunciation guide, the part of speech, and a brief definition. I wrote these definitions with the idea of keeping them simple and nontechnical. Some vocabulary texts provide complicated dictionary definitions that include words students do not know; I've tried to make the definitions as friendly and as useful as possible.
- **Words to Watch:** This new section asks students to pick 3–5 words they may be having trouble with and write their own sentences using the words. This section is an additional chance for students to grasp the meaning of a few words that may be difficult for them.

ADDITIONAL FEATURES

In addition to the features described above, the text includes several sections that will aid students in vocabulary acquisition. The other elements of the text include the following:

- **Getting Started:** The text begins with a Getting Started chapter, which helps familiarize students with some of the tools of vocabulary acquisition. The "Parts of Speech" section within this chapter gives sample words and sentences for the eight parts of speech. "Using the Dictionary" dissects a sample dictionary entry and provides an exercise on using guide words. "Completing Analogies" explains how analogies work, provides sample analogies, and gives students analogy exercises to complete. This section will prepare students for the analogy Self-Tests contained in several chapters of the text. The "Benefits of Flash Cards" section encourages students to make flash cards beginning with Chapter 1. The page explains the advantages of using flash cards and makes students aware of the "Create Your Own Flash Cards" section at the end of the text.
- **Word Parts:** The three Word Parts chapters introduce prefixes, roots, and suffixes used throughout the book. Students learn the meanings of these forms, and sample words illustrate the forms. Self-Tests in each Word Parts chapter give students the opportunity to practice using the word parts.
- **Review Chapters:** Three Review chapters focus on the preceding seven or eight chapters. They divide the words into different activity groups and test students' cumulative knowledge. The words appear in artistic, test, written, puzzle, and dramatic formats. These repeated and varied exposures increase the likelihood that the students will remember the words, not for one chapter or a test, but for life.
- **Create Your Own Flash Cards:** The Create Your Own Flash Cards section teaches students how to make and use flash cards. Students can use the cards for self-study. Additionally, instructors can use them for the supplemental activities and games provided in the Instructor's Manual. Flash card templates are included in the back of the text. Students can photocopy the blank pages if they want to use this format or they can use index cards as described in the Flash Card directions.
- **Word List:** The inside back cover features a list of all the vocabulary words and the page number on which the definition is given. A list of the word parts from the Word Parts chapters is also included on the inside back cover with page references.
- **Pronunciation Key:** On the inside front cover is a pronunciation key to help students understand the pronunciation symbols used in this text. The inside front cover also offers some additional guidelines on pronunciation issues.

FEATURES NEW TO THIS EDITION

This edition of the text has several new features in response to instructor comments. The new materials and organization of the book have been employed to make the text more appealing to students and easier for instructors to use.

- **Refined In-Chapter Organization**: The Word List is now at the end of each chapter, so students can do the Predicting exercise without accidentally looking at the Word List below. The last page of each chapter contains the Word List and the Words to Watch exercise. Instructors can now have students tear out the Self-Tests to hand in and not lose the thematic reading for the next chapter.
- **Added Content**: Hints have been added to each chapter to deal with more learning situations students face. The new Words to Watch exercise gives students extra practice with words that are difficult for them. A list of the Word Parts introduced in the text has been added to the Word List on the inside back cover, so instructors and students can easily find a word part they want to review.
- **New Readings**: Over half of the chapters have new readings in either topics or formats more likely to appeal to students. Part II includes the new theme, The Unusual. Additionally, new words have been added to some chapters. Photographs have also been added to several of the readings for more visually friendly chapters.
- **New Predicting Exercise Format**: Students will now write out the definition from a choice of five definitions instead of picking from a three-part multiple-choice answer. Writing the definition will help students better remember the meaning of a word.
- **Updated Analogies Section**: The Analogies Appendix has been moved to the Getting Started chapter to allow students a chance to work with analogies before they start the Self-Tests. The section has been renamed "Completing Analogies," and it offers greater explanation on how to complete analogies and offers practice exercises.
- **Updated CD-ROM**: The CD-ROM that accompanies *Interactive Vocabulary* has been updated to include more effective and relevant exercises.

THE TEACHING AND LEARNING PACKAGE

Each component of the teaching and learning package for *Interactive Vocabulary* has been carefully crafted to maximize the main text's value.

- **Instructor's Manual and Test Bank**: The Instructor's Manual and Test Bank, which is almost as long as the main text, includes options for additional Collaborative Activities and games. The collaborative section explains ways students can share their work on the Interactive Exercises in pairs, in small groups, or with the whole class. Ideas for other collaborative activities using different learning styles are also offered. The games section presents games that can be used with individual chapters or for review of several chapters. Some of the games are individual; others are full-class activities. Some games have winners, and some are just for fun. The games may involve acting, drawing, or writing. The Collaborative Activities and games give students the opportunity to use the words in conversational settings and a chance to work with others.

  The Test Bank, formatted for easy copying, includes two tests for each chapter as well as combined tests of two to three chapters. There are also Mastery Tests to accompany the Review chapters and full-book Mastery Tests that can be used as final exams. ISBN: 0-321-39329-5.
- *Interactive Vocabulary* **Study Wizard CD-ROM**: In the computer age many students enjoy learning via computers. Available with this text is the *Interactive Vocabulary* Study Wizard CD-ROM, which features additional exercises and tests that provide for even more interaction between the students and the words. The CD-ROM has an audio component that allows students to hear each chapter's thematic reading and the pronunciation of each word as often as they choose. Students are often reluctant to use the new words they learn

© 2007 Pearson Education, Inc.

because they aren't sure how to pronounce them. The pronunciation guides in each chapter do help to address this fear, but actually hearing the words spoken will give students greater confidence in using the words. Contact your Longman publishing representative to order the student text packaged with the CD-ROM for an additional $3.00.

FOR ADDITIONAL READING AND REFERENCE

The Longman Basic Skills Package

In addition to the book-specific supplements discussed above, many other skills-based supplements are available for both instructors and students. All of these supplements are available either free or at greatly reduced prices.

- **The Dictionary Deal**. Two dictionaries can be shrink-wrapped with *Interactive Vocabulary* at a nominal fee. *The New American Webster Handy College Dictionary* is a paperback reference text with more than 100,000 entries. *Merriam-Webster's Collegiate Dictionary*, eleventh edition, is a hardback reference with a citation file of more than 14.5 million examples of English words drawn from actual use. For more information on how to shrink-wrap a dictionary with your text, please contact your Longman publishing representative.
- **Longman Vocabulary Web Site**. For additional vocabulary-related resources, visit our free vocabulary Web site at **http://www.ablongman.com/vocabulary.**

ACKNOWLEDGMENTS

I would like to thank the following reviewers for their helpful suggestions for this third edition:

Ivan G. Dole, North Lake College
Beth Hash, Bluefield State College
Debra Herrera, Cisco Jr. College
Joyce Jacobs, Lee College
Miriam Kinard, Trident Technical College
Robert H. Ludwiczak, Texas A&M University
Kelly Lyon, University of Central Arkansas
Ann Ritter, Baltimore City Community College
Dianne Ruggiero, Broward Community College
Rebecca Suarez, University of Texas–El Paso

Additionally, I want to thank Frederick Speers, Associate Editor of Basic Skills at Longman, for his help in organizing this edition. Thanks also to the Supplement and Marketing sections of Longman for their efforts on various aspects of the book. I want to thank my colleagues over the years for their support and enlightening discussions. Finally, I want to express my gratitude to my family. They have encouraged me in whatever endeavors I have undertaken—a confidence that I greatly appreciate.

I am proud to present the third edition of a book that continues to make learning vocabulary fun and fruitful.

—AMY E. OLSEN

ALSO AVAILABLE

Book 2 of the Vocabulary Series:
Active Vocabulary: General and Academic Words by Amy E. Olsen

Book 3 of the Vocabulary Series:
Academic Vocabulary: Academic Words by Amy E. Olsen

TO THE STUDENT

This book is designed to make learning vocabulary fun. You will increase the benefits of this book if you keep a few points in mind:

1. **Interact with the words**. Each chapter contains nine exposures to a word, and your instructor may introduce one or two additional activities. If you're careful in your reading and thorough in doing the activities for each chapter, learning the words will be fun and easy.

2. **Appreciate the importance of words**. The words for the readings were picked from magazines, newspapers, novels, and lists of words likely to appear on standardized tests (such as SAT, GRE). These are words you will encounter in the classroom and in everyday life. Learning these words will help you be a more informed citizen and make your academic life much richer. Even if you don't currently have an interest in one of the readings, keep an open mind: the words may appear in the article you read in tomorrow's newspaper or on an exam in one of next semester's classes. The readings also come in different formats as a reminder that you can learn new vocabulary anywhere, from an interview to a journal entry.

3. **Find your preferred learning style**. The book aims to provide exercises for all types of learners—visual, aural, and interpersonal. But only you can say which learning style works best for you. See which activities (drawings, acting, matching, completing stories) you like most, and replicate those activities when they aren't part of the chapter.

4. **Value critical thinking**. The variety of exercise formats you will find in the following pages make the book fun to work with and build a range of critical thinking skills. For example, the analogies will help you see relationships between words, the fill-in-the-blank formats will aid you in learning to put words in context, and the True/False Self-Tests will focus your attention on whether words are used correctly in a sentence. Each type of activity will be developing your critical thinking skills while building your vocabulary.

5. **Remember that learning is fun**. Don't make a chore out of learning new words, or any other new skill for that matter. If you enjoy what you're doing, you're more likely to welcome the information and to retain it.

Enjoy your journey through *Interactive Vocabulary!*

—AMY E. OLSEN

© 2007 Pearson Education, Inc.

Getting Started

There are eight parts of speech. A word's part of speech is based on how it is used in a sentence. Words can, therefore, be more than one part of speech. For an example, note how the word *punch* is used below.

nouns: (n.) name a person, place, or thing

EXAMPLES: Ms. Lopez, New Orleans, lamp, warmth

Ms. Lopez enjoyed her *trip* to *New Orleans* where she bought a beautiful *lamp*. The *warmth* of the *sun* filled *Claire* with *happiness*. I drank five *cups* of the orange *punch*.

pronouns: (pron.) take the place of a noun

EXAMPLES: I, me, you, she, he, it, her, him, we, they, which, that, anybody, everybody

Everybody liked the music at the party. *It* was the kind that made people want to dance. *They* bought a new car, *which* hurt their bank account.

verbs: (v.) express an action or state of being

EXAMPLES: enjoy, run, think, read, dance, am, is, are, was, were

Lily *read* an interesting book yesterday. I *am* tired. He *is* an excellent student. She *punched* the bully.

adjectives: (adj.) modify (describe or explain) a noun or pronoun

EXAMPLES: pretty, old, two, expensive, red, small

The *old* car was covered with *red* paint on *one* side. The *two* women met for lunch at an *expensive* restaurant. The *punch* bowl was empty soon after Uncle Al got to the party.

adverbs: (adv.) modify a verb, an adjective, or another adverb

EXAMPLES: very, shortly, first, too, soon, quickly, finally, furthermore, however

We will meet *shortly* after one o'clock. The *very* pretty dress sold *quickly*. I liked her; *however*, there was something strange about her.

prepositions: (prep.) placed before a noun or pronoun to make a phrase that relates to other parts of the sentence

EXAMPLES: after, around, at, before, by, from, in, into, of, off, on, through, to, up, with

He told me to be *at* his house *around* noon. You must go *through* all the steps to do the job.

conjunctions: (conj.) join words or other sentence elements and show a relationship between the connected items

EXAMPLES: and, but, or, nor, for, so, yet, after, although, because, if, since, than, when

I went to the movies, *and* I went to dinner on Tuesday. I will not go to the party this weekend *because* I have to study. I don't want to hear your reasons *or* excuses.

interjections: (interj.) show surprise or emotion

EXAMPLES: oh, hey, wow, ah, ouch

Oh, I forgot to do my homework! *Wow*, I got an A on the test!

© 2007 Pearson Education, Inc.

USING THE DICTIONARY

There will be times when you need to use a dictionary for one of its many features; becoming familiar with dictionary **entries** will make using a dictionary more enjoyable. The words in a dictionary are arranged alphabetically. The words on a given page are signaled by **guide words** at the top of the page. If the word you are looking for comes alphabetically between these two words then your word is on that page.

Guide words

Entry

1436

wing tip *n* (ca. 1908) **1 a** : the edge or outer margin of a bird's wing **b** *usu* **wingtip** : the outer end of an airplane wing **2** : a toe cap having a point that extends back toward the throat of the shoe and curving sides that extend toward the shank **3** : a shoe having a wing tip

¹wink \'wiŋk\ *vb* [ME, fr. OE *wincian;* akin to OHG *winchan* to stagger, wink and perh. to L *vacillare* to sway, Skt *vañcati* he goes crookedly] *vi* (bef. 12c) **1** : to shut one eye briefly as a signal or in teasing **2** : to close and open the eyelids quickly **3** : to avoid seeing or noting something — usu. used with *at* **4** : to gleam or flash intermittently: TWINKLE <her glasses *~ing* in the sunlight — Harper Lee> **5 a** : to come to an end — usu. used with *out* **b** : to stop shining — usu. used with *out* **6** : to signal a message with a light ~ *vt* **1** : to cause to open and shut **2** : to affect or influence by or as if by blinking the eyes

²wink *n* (14c) **1** : a brief period of sleep : NAP <catching a ~> **2 a** : a hint or sign given by winking **b** : an act of winking **3** : the time of a wink: INSTANT <quick as a ~> **4** : a flicker of the eyelids: BLINK

wink·er \'wiŋ-kər\ *n* (1549) **1** : one that winks **2** : a horse's blinder

¹win·kle \'wiŋ-kəl\ *n* [by shortening] (1585) : ²PERIWINKLE

²winkle *vi* **win·kled; win·kling** \-k(ə-)liŋ\ [freq. of *wink*] (1791): TWINKLE

³winkle *vt* **win·kled; win·kling** \-k(ə-)liŋ\ [¹*winkle;* fr. the process of extracting a winkle from its shell] (1918) **1** *chiefly Brit* : to displace, remove, or evict from a position — usu. used with *out* **2** *chiefly Brit* : to obtain or draw out by effort — usu. used with *out* <no attempt to ~ out why they do it — Joan Bakewell>

win·ner \'wi-nər\ *n* (14c) : one that wins: as **a** : one that is successful esp. through praiseworthy ability and hard work **b** : a victor esp. in games and sports **c** : one that wins admiration **d** : a shot in a court game that is not returned and that scores for the player making it

---

win·ter·ize \'win-tə-,rīz\ *vt* **-ized ; -iz·ing** (1934) : to make ready for winter or winter use and esp. resistant or proof against winter weather <~ a car> — **win·ter·i·za·tion** \,win-tə-rə-'zā-shən\ *n*

win·ter—kill \'win-tər-,kil\ *vt* (ca. 1806) : to kill (as a plant) by exposure to winter conditions ~ *vi* : to die as a result of exposure to winter conditions — **winterkill** *n*

win·ter·ly \'win-tər-lē\ *adj* (1559) : of, relating to, or occurring in winter : WINTRY

winter melon *n* (ca. 1900) **1** : any of several muskmelons (as a casaba or honeydew melon) that are fruits of a cultivated vine (*Cucumis melo indorus*) **2** : a large white-fleshed melon that is the fruit of an Asian vine (*Benincasa hispida*) and is used esp. in Chinese cooking

winter quarters *n pl but sing or pl in constr* (1641) : a winter residence or station (as of a military unit or a circus)

winter savory *n* (1597) : a perennial European mint (*Satureja montana*) with leaves used for seasoning — compare SUMMER SAVORY

winter squash *n* (1775) : any of various hard-shelled squashes that belong to cultivars derived from several species (esp. *Cucurbita maxima, C. moschata,* and *C. pepo*) and that can be stored for several months

win·ter·tide \'win-tər-,tīd\ *n* (bef. 12c) : WINTERTIME

win·ter·time \-,tīm\ *n* (14c) : the season of winter

win through *vi* (1644) : to survive difficulties and reach a desired or satisfactory end <*win through* to a better life beyond — B. F. Reilly>

win·tle \'wi-nᵊl, 'win-tᵊl\ *vi* **win·tled; win·tling** \'win(t)-liŋ; 'wi-nᵊl-iŋ, 'win-tᵊl-\ [perh. fr. D dial. *windtelen* to reel] (1786) **1** *Scot* : STAGGER, REEL **2** *Scot* : WRIGGLE

win·try \'win-trē\ *also* **win·tery** \'win-t(ə-)rē\ *adj* **win·tri·er; -est** (bef. 12c) **1** : of, relating to, or characteristic of winter **2 a** : weathered by or as if by winter : AGED, HOARY **b** : CHEERLESS, CHILLING <a ~ greeting> — **win·tri·ness** \'win-trē-nəs\ *n*

SOURCE: By permission. From *Merriam-Webster's Collegiate® Dictionary, Eleventh Edition* © 2004 by Merriam-Webster, Incorporated (www.Merriam-Webster.com).

2 GETTING STARTED

Most dictionaries contain the following information in an entry:

- The **pronunciation**—symbols show how a word should be spoken, including how the word is divided into syllables and where the stress should be placed on a word. The Pronunciation Key for this book is located on the inside front cover. The key shows the symbols used to indicate the sound of a word. Every dictionary has a pronunciation method, and a pronunciation key or guide is usually found in the front pages, with a partial key at the bottom of each page. The differences in the pronunciation systems used by dictionaries are usually slight.
- The **part of speech**—usually abbreviated, such as *n.* for noun, *v.* for verb, and *adj.* for adjective. A key to these abbreviations and others is usually found in the front of the dictionary.
- The **definition**—usually the most common meaning is listed first followed by other meanings.
- An **example of the word in a sentence**—the sentence is usually in italics and follows each meaning.
- **Synonyms** and **antonyms**—*synonyms* are words with similar meanings, and *antonyms* are words that mean the opposite. (You should also consider owning a **thesaurus,** a book that lists synonyms and antonyms.)
- The **etymology**—the history of a word, usually including the language(s) it came from.
- The **spelling of different forms** of the word—these forms may include unusual plurals and verb tenses (especially irregular forms).

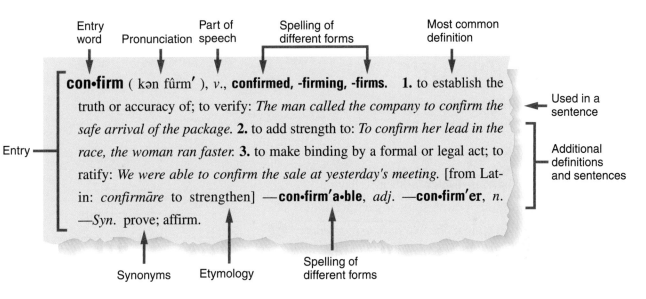

When choosing a dictionary, take the time to look at different dictionaries and see what appeals to you. Dictionaries come in several sizes and are made for different purposes. First read some of the entries and see if the definitions make sense to you. See which of the features above are used in the dictionary. Is it important to you to be able to study the etymology of a word? Would you like sample sentences? Some dictionaries have illustrations in the margins. Decide if that is a feature you would use. Check to see if the print is large enough for you to read easily.

Decide on how you will use this dictionary. Do you want a paperback dictionary to put in your backpack? Or is this going to be the dictionary for your desk and a large hardback version would be the better choice? Several disciplines have specialized dictionaries with meanings that apply to those fields, such as law or medicine. There are also bilingual dictionaries, such as French/English or Spanish/English that can be helpful for school or travel. Take time in picking out your dictionary because a good dictionary will be a companion for years to come. A few dictionaries to consider are *Merriam-Webster's Collegiate Dictionary, The American Heritage Dictionary, The Random House College Dictionary,* and *The Oxford Dictionary.*

In general, when you are reading try to use context clues, the words around the word you don't know, to first figure out the meaning of a word, but if you are still in doubt don't hesitate to refer to a dictionary for the exact definition. Don't forget that dictionaries also contain more than definitions and are an essential reference source for any student.

© 2007 Pearson Education, Inc.

USING GUIDE WORDS

Use the sample guide words to determine on which page each of the ten words will be found. Write the page number next to the entry word.

Page	Guide Words
157	bone/boo
159	boot/born
435	endemic/endorse
654	humanist/humongous
655	humor/hunter
975	pamphlet/pandemonium
976	pander/pant
1480	velvet/venom

EXAMPLE: _654_ humdinger

_____ 1. pane

_____ 2. panda

_____ 3. bonnet

_____ 4. vendor

_____ 5. ending

_____ 6. Hungarian

_____ 7. borax

_____ 8. pandowdy

_____ 9. humid

_____ 10. humble

ENTRY IDENTIFICATION

Label the parts of the following entry:

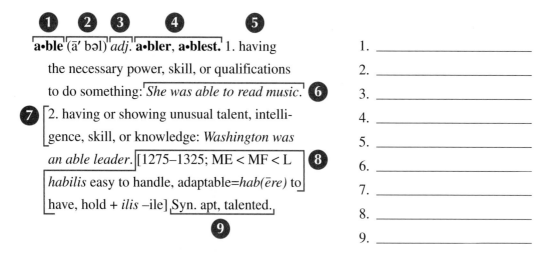

1 **2** **3** **4** **5**

a•ble (ā′ bəl) *adj.* **a•bler, a•blest.** 1. having the necessary power, skill, or qualifications to do something: *She was able to read music.* **6**
7 2. having or showing unusual talent, intelligence, skill, or knowledge: *Washington was an able leader.* [1275–1325; ME < MF < L **8** *habilis* easy to handle, adaptable=*hab(ēre)* to have, hold + *ilis* –ile] Syn. apt, talented.
9

1. _____

2. _____

3. _____

4. _____

5. _____

6. _____

7. _____

8. _____

9. _____

COMPLETING ANALOGIES

An **analogy** shows a relationship between words. Working with analogies helps one to see connections between items, which is a crucial critical thinking skill. Analogies are written as follows: "big : large :: fast : quick." The colon (:) means *is to*. The analogy reads "big *is to* large as fast *is to* quick." To complete analogies

1. find a relationship between the first pair of words
2. look for a similar relationship in another set of words

In the example above *big* and *large* have similar meanings; they are synonyms. *Fast* and *quick* also have similar meanings, so the relationship between the four words uses synonyms.

Common relationships used in analogies (with examples) include

synonyms (trip : journey)	grammatical structure (shaking : shivering)
antonyms (real : fake)	cause and effect (step in a puddle : get wet)
examples (strawberry : fruit)	sequences (turn on car : drive)
part to a whole (handle : cup)	an object to a user or its use (spatula : chef)

Analogies in this book come in matching and fill-in-the-blank forms. Try the following analogies for practice.

MATCHING

1. old : young :: _____   a. preface : book

2. clip coupons :: go shopping _____   b. put on shoes : take a walk

3. peel : banana :: _____   c. low wages : strike

4. no rain : drought :: _____   d. rested : tired

FILL-IN-THE-BLANK

writer	passion	abduct	sadly

5. frozen : chilled :: kidnap : _____

6. interrupting : rude :: embracing : _____

7. slow : slowly :: sad : _____

8. baton : conductor :: computer : _____

© 2007 Pearson Education, Inc.

1. To figure out this analogy first one needs to see that *old* and *young* are opposites or **antonyms.** Next look at the choices and see if another pair of words are antonyms, and, yes, *rested* and *tired* are opposites. The answer is d.
2. A person would *clip coupons* and then *go shopping,* so there is a **sequence** of events. Of the choices, one would *put on shoes* and then *take a walk,* another sequence. The answer is b.
3. A *peel* is a part of a *banana,* while a *preface* is part of a *book,* so the connection is **part to a whole.** The answer is a.
4. When an area gets *no rain* it can lead to a *drought,* and when people get paid *low wages,* they can go on *strike.* The connection among these pairs is **cause and effect.** The answer is c.
5. *Frozen* and *chilled* have similar meanings; they are **synonyms.** To solve the analogy, pick a word that has a similar meaning to *kidnap,* which would be *abduct.*
6. *Interrupting* a person is **an example** of a *rude behavior. Embracing* is an example of another type of behavior; in this case, it fits as an example of *passion.*
7. *Slow* is an adjective and *slowly* an adverb; *sad* is an adjective and *sadly* an adverb. This analogy works by using the same **grammatical structure** between the words.
8. A *baton* is used by a *conductor.* Who uses a *computer?* Among the choices, a *writer* obviously fits. The relationship here is **object to user.**

Sometimes you may come up with a relationship between the first two words that makes sense, but doesn't fit any of the choices. Look at the choices and the two words again to see if you can find a way any four words fit together. Also do any obvious matches first, and with fewer choices it will be easier to spot the harder connections. Doing analogies can be fun as you begin to make clever connections and see word relationships in new ways. Finding word connections will help your brain make other connections in areas as diverse as writing essays, doing math problems, and arranging travel plans. Analogies are just another way to exercise your thinking skills.

Try a few more analogies and check your answers on page 10 to see how you did.

MATCHING

1. button : shirt ::   _____   a. broom : janitor

2. map : traveler ::   _____   b. drawer : desk

3. calm : tranquil ::   _____   c. stayed up late : exhausted

4. watched a comedy : laughed ::   _____   d. wise : smart

FILL-IN-THE-BLANK

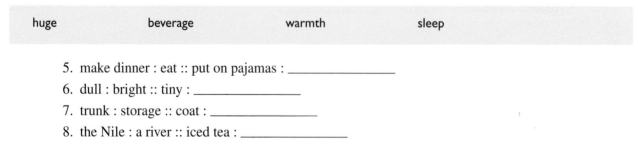

| huge | beverage | warmth | sleep |

5. make dinner : eat :: put on pajamas : _____
6. dull : bright :: tiny : _____
7. trunk : storage :: coat : _____
8. the Nile : a river :: iced tea : _____

BENEFITS OF FLASH CARDS

There are several benefits to using flash cards to help you study vocabulary words.

Making the Cards   The first benefit comes from just making the cards. When you make a card, you will practice writing the word and its definition. You may also write a sentence using the word, record its part of speech, or draw a picture of the word. See the section "Create Your Own Flash Cards" on page 164 at the back of this book for ideas on how to make flash cards. Creating the cards allows for a personal experience with the words, which makes learning the words easier.

Working with Others   Another benefit is that using the cards can lead to collaborative activities. When you ask a friend, family member, or classmate to quiz you on the words, you get the chance to work with someone else, which many people enjoy. You may even establish a study group with the friends you find from quizzing each other on your flash cards.

Evaluating Your Learning   A third benefit is that the cards serve as pre-tests that let you evaluate how well you know a word. When a friend quizzes you, ask him or her to go over the words you miss several times. As the stack of flash cards with words you don't know gets smaller, you know that the words are becoming part of your vocabulary. You know that you are prepared to face a word on a quiz or test when you can correctly give the definition several times.

Making and using the flash cards should be fun. Enjoy the process of learning new words. Turn to the back of the book now to review the directions for creating flash cards, and you will be ready to make cards beginning with Chapter 1. You can use the templates provided at the end of the book to get started.

© 2007 Pearson Education, Inc.

CHAPTER 1 Vocabulary Growth

Finding the Right Words

No one can **predict** what vocabulary words one will need to know in the future, but it is assured that a well-developed vocabulary will lead to increased success in life. Through **diligent** work anyone can improve his or her vocabulary. All it takes is time and careful study.

    Key concepts in vocabulary growth: 5

1. *Read.* Words are best learned through reading. Look for **context clues** as you read. Context clues are the words around a word that give hints about its meaning. Context clues may be a **synonym** (a word with a similar meaning to another word), an **antonym** (a word that means the opposite of a word), and examples of a word. The general meaning of   10 the whole sentence or paragraph can also be a context clue that helps you understand an unknown word.

2. *Use* ***phonics*** *to sound out a word.* Sometimes you think you might not know a word when you read it, but if you say it out loud you may discover that you do know the word. You can refer to a dictionary to find out how to pronounce a word.   15

3. *Make connections.* Be **interactive** with the words you want to learn. Make your learning a two-way communication by creating flash cards, drawing pictures of the words, and using new words in your writing and speech. Think of a **theme** to write about and use the words you are studying in an essay, note, e-mail, or journal. For example, your theme might be about what a good day you had at school or the problems you are encountering at your job or in your love life. Focus on a topic and   20 have fun incorporating new words into your writing.

4. *Work with others.* **Collaborative** activities can be fun and help you remember a subject better. There are a lot of ways to work with other people, but a couple of ideas are to meet with a friend and quiz each other using your flash cards or have a conversation   25 with a classmate where you each use five of the words you are studying. Also consider creating a study group to keep you motivated.

    Learning vocabulary is like reading a mystery novel. When reading a mystery, you look for clues, you interact with the plot,   30 you try different solutions, and eventually you discover who did it. The **analogy** works when you do the same with your vocabulary studies: look for context clues, interact with the words, try different meanings, and eventually find the right one. You will also discover that as your vocabulary grows reading will be more fun, and it will be easier to find the right   35 words to use in your writing and speech.

▌▌▌▌ PREDICTING

For each set, write the definition on the line next to the word to which it belongs. If you are unsure, return to the reading on page 8, and underline any context clues you find. After you've made your predictions, check your answers against the Word List on page 13. Place a checkmark in the box next to each word whose definition you missed. These are the words you'll want to study closely.

SET ONE

word with a similar meaning	word that means the opposite	careful	to tell in advance

words around another word that give hints about its meaning

- ❑ 1. **predict** (line 1) _____
- ❑ 2. **diligent** (line 3) _____
- ❑ 3. **context clues** (line 6) _____
- ❑ 4. **synonym** (line 8) _____
- ❑ 5. **antonym** (line 9) _____

SET TWO

a reading method in which letters are associated with their sounds	a focused topic
working with other people	making connections	a comparison

- ❑ 6. **phonics** (line 13) _____
- ❑ 7. **interactive** (line 16) _____
- ❑ 8. **theme** (line 18) _____
- ❑ 9. **collaborative** (line 22) _____
- ❑ 10. **analogy** (line 32) _____

▌▌▌▌ SELF-TESTS

1 For each set complete the analogies. See Completing Analogies on page 5 for instructions and practice. Use each word once.

SET ONE

VOCABULARY LIST

collaborative	phonics	context clues	analogy	diligent

1. combine : join :: energetic : _____
2. traffic jam : got home late :: used _____ : pronounced a word easier
3. shampoo : to clean hair :: _____ : to show comparison
4. eating a whole turkey : hungry :: building a house together : _____
5. petal : flower :: _____ : paragraph

© 2007 Pearson Education, Inc.

VOCABULARY LIST

interactive	antonym	theme	synonyms	predict

6. loud : noisy :: _____ : specific topic

7. a person enters a running race : compete :: a person says in October that the Dolphins will win the Superbowl : _____

8. a mansion : huge :: a computer game : _____

9. kind : cruel :: synonym : _____

10. bike racer : helmet :: writer : _____

2 Pick the best word from the list below to complete the sentence. Use each word once.

VOCABULARY LIST

synonym	interactive	theme	collaborative	antonyms
diligent	analogy	phonics	predict	context clues

1. I went to see a fortune-teller to hear her _____ whether I would be rich someday.

2. The _____ for our first paper in English class was technology.

3. I listened to ten _____ tapes in the reading lab to improve my pronunciation.

4. The student made an interesting _____ between writing a paper and riding a bike.

5. The woman wanted to become an executive in the company, so she was _____ at her job.

6. Making a movie is a _____ project because it involves writers, actors, technicians, and the director to put it together.

7. When I am reading and come across a word I don't know, I look for _____ to help me figure out the meaning.

8. Using a computer can be _____ because some programs tell you if your answer is right or wrong, and then you can think about your choices and make changes.

9. When I want to stop repeating the same word in a paper, but I need another word with the same meaning, I look in a thesaurus to find a _____.

10. *Stubborn* and *flexible* are important _____ to learn. I discovered the difference between the two when my friends told me to stop being stubborn and start being more flexible or they wouldn't see me anymore.

3 Circle the word that correctly completes each sentence.

1. By using (antonyms, phonics) I can usually correctly pronounce new words.

2. I didn't like (diligent, collaborative) projects until I met my boyfriend while working on a history class assignment with him.

Answers to the analogies practice in the Getting Started section on page 6:
1. b 2. a 3. d 4. c 5. sleep 5. huge 6. warmth 7. beverage

---

3. I tried to (predict, interactive) what my biology teacher would ask on the exam, and I did a good job—I knew all but two of the questions.

4. I have found that using (phonics, synonyms) has made my writing more interesting to read.

5. Now that I am aware of (phonics, context clues) I can figure out the meaning of unknown words more easily.

6. I was so (diligent, collaborative) about doing my homework on Friday that I was able to go to the party on Saturday.

7. My sister made the (analogy, phonics) that her vacation was like spending a week in a life raft. After hearing about all the problems she had, I think she was right.

8. I like my Spanish class because the professor makes it (diligent, interactive); we participate in some way every day.

9. The (antonym, theme) for my first speech is how to improve the college.

10. My friend described the cake as tasty, but I can think of several (antonyms, analogies) that would fit it better: horrid, rotten, gross.

4 Answer each question by writing the vocabulary word on the line next to the example it best fits. Use each word once.

VOCABULARY LIST

analogy	collaborative	diligent	phonics	synonyms
interactive	predicting	antonyms	theme	context clues

1. *Cold, freezing,* and *chilly* are what type of words for hot? _____

2. Keri proofreads her papers six times. What kind of student is she? _____

3. After he looks at the clouds, Matt says it is going to rain. What is he doing? _____

4. Tony announces that the topic of the meeting is "how to raise funds for a club trip." What is he providing for the meeting? _____

5. June says, "Life is one big tea party." What kind of comparison has she made? _____

6. *Warm, boiling,* and *sweltering* are what type of words for hot? _____

7. Milt looks up *chrome* in the dictionary and finds the pronunciation krōm. What is he using to help him pronounce the word? _____

8. When a brother and sister help each other pick up their toys, what are they being?

_____

9. Katy connects her history lecture to a short story she read in English. What type of learning is she using? _____

10. Dan says, "I am famished. I haven't eaten anything since yesterday." If you use the sentence "I haven't eaten anything since yesterday" to figure out the meaning of *famished,* what have you benefited from? _____

© 2007 Pearson Education, Inc.

▮▮▮▮ INTERACTIVE EXERCISE

Write a note to a classmate about the benefits of increasing one's vocabulary. Use at least five of the vocabulary words introduced in this chapter. Draft your note below.

Dear _____,

_____

_____

_____

_____

_____

_____

_____

_____

_____

Sincerely,

_____

HINT

Flash Card Reminder

Flash cards are an excellent way to study vocabulary. Turn to the "Create Your Own Flash Cards" section (page 164) for suggestions on ways to make and use flash cards. Remember to carry your flash cards with you and study for at least a few minutes each day. Also ask classmates, friends, and family members to quiz you using the flash cards. There are a few templates to get you started at the end of this book. Make copies of them before you fill them all out if you want to use them for all the chapters in this book.

▌▌▌▌ WORD LIST

analogy
[ə nal′ ə jē]
n. a comparison; likeness

antonym
[an′ tə nim]
n. word that means the opposite

collaborative
[kə lab′ ûr ə tiv′]
adj. working together; working with other people

context clues
[kon′ tekst klooz′]
n. words around another word that give hints about its meaning

diligent
[dil′ ə jənt]
adj. steady and energetic; careful

interactive
[in′ tûr ak′ tiv]
adj. making connections; permits two-way communication

phonics
[fon′ iks]
n. a reading method in which letters are associated with their sounds or pronunciation

predict
[pri dikt′]
v. to tell in advance

synonym
[sin′ ə nim]
n. word with a similar meaning

theme
[thēm]
n. a specific or focused subject or topic

▌▌▌▌ WORDS TO WATCH

Which words would you like to practice with a bit more? Pick 3–5 words to study and list them below. Write the word, its definition, and compose your own sentence using the word correctly. This extra practice could be the final touch to learning a word.

Word	Definition	Your Sentence
1. _____	_____	_____
_____	_____	_____
2. _____	_____	_____
_____	_____	_____
3. _____	_____	_____
_____	_____	_____
4. _____	_____	_____
_____	_____	_____
5. _____	_____	_____
_____	_____	_____

© 2007 Pearson Education, Inc.

2 College Life

An Exciting Start

Juanita was the first person in her family to go to college. Her family had moved to California from Mexico when she was two years old. She was excited but also nervous
5 about entering college. She knew that getting an education would **empower** her to get a better job. With hope and fear, she headed off to the college for **orientation.**

At the orientation workshop a **counselor**
10 told her and the other students how to select classes, what tests they needed to take, and what services the college provided to help them succeed. Juanita had to take **assessment** tests in English and math to see what level class she should start at. After the general meeting, Juanita met with a counselor.

15 "Juanita, do you know what you want to **major** in? What are your interests?" asked Ms. Maxwell.

"I'm not sure. I do like math and art."

"We have excellent **faculty** who teach in both areas. You should take classes in both subjects and get to know the professors; they can help you make up your mind. You don't have to **declare** your major right away. You can wait until you have a clear idea of what you want to study before you formally
20 tell the college. I would also suggest taking an **aptitude** test to see what areas you may have special talents in."

"Thank you for talking with me, Ms. Maxwell. I feel I can better **cope** with college after coming to today's orientation."

"You have made a **commitment** to your future by coming today, and I am sure you will be able to
25 deal with the pressures of college. But if you ever need any assistance don't hesitate to come to this office for help."

Juanita left the college excited and no longer nervous about her new environment.

▌▌▌▌ PREDICTING

For each set, write the definition on the line next to the word to which it belongs. If you are unsure, return to the reading on page 14, and underline any context clues you find. After you've made your predictions, check your answers against the Word List on page 19. Place a checkmark in the box next to each word whose definition you missed. These are the words you'll want to study closely.

SET ONE

testing	advisor	the principal area of study chosen by a student in college
to enable	a program to help people adapt to a new environment

❑ 1. **empower** (line 6) _____

❑ 2. **orientation** (line 8) _____

❑ 3. **counselor** (line 9) _____

❑ 4. **assessment** (line 13) _____

❑ 5. **major** (line 15) _____

SET TWO

to survive	to announce formally	teachers	a promise	talent

❑ 6. **faculty** (line 17) _____

❑ 7. **declare** (line 18) _____

❑ 8. **aptitude** (line 20) _____

❑ 9. **cope** (line 22) _____

❑ 10. **commitment** (line 24) _____

▌▌▌▌ SELF-TESTS

1 In each group, circle the word that does not have a connection to the other three words.

EXAMPLE: ability   faculty   (helplessness)   power

When you have the faculty to do something, you have the ability or power. *Helplessness* is not related to the other words.

1. instructors	faculty	teachers	students
2. handle	survive	fail	cope
3. promise	pledge	commitment	uncertainty
4. talent	intelligence	inability	aptitude
5. permit	refuse	enable	empower
6. major	serious	minor	principal

© 2007 Pearson Education, Inc.

7. announce	declare	assert	suppress
8. advisor	counselor	opponent	guide
9. conclusion	introduction	program	orientation
10. testing	plunge	assessment	evaluation

2 Juanita is taking classes in France for a year. Fill in the blanks of her letter to her parents with the appropriate vocabulary word. Use each word once.

VOCABULARY LIST

cope	assessment	counselor	faculty	major
orientation	declare	empowered	aptitude	commitment

Dear Mom and Dad,

The semester is going well. I am really happy with my (1)_____; International Business suits me well. We had an excellent (2)_____ to the program during the first week. They told us about our classes and took us on a city tour of Paris to become familiar with the city. The (3)_____ test I took before I came over put me in the right level of French. I understand most of what the professor says. The (4)_____ here are great. They are friendly and helpful with the course work and with understanding a different culture. I am taking a cooking class for fun and have found I have quite the (5)_____ for making crepes. I can't wait to cook for you when I get home. At first it was a little hard to (6)_____ with the differences in cultures, especially hearing French all day, but now it is not that hard. Thank you for your (7)_____ to my education. Your help has made this trip possible. Next week I go to the (8)_____ to get advice on what classes to take next semester. This experience has (9)_____ me to go on to graduate school. I want to get a Master's in Business Administration next. You might think that is a lot to (10)_____ after eight weeks in France, but I know I can do it. I hope all is well at home. I will write more later.

Love,

Juanita

3 Put a T for true or F for false next to each statement.

_____ 1. Learning to read will not empower a person to do better in school.

_____ 2. It can be hard to cope with planning a wedding.

_____ 3. A candidate needs to declare that he or she is running for office.

_____ 4. The faculty at most colleges usually have no more than a high school education.

_____ 5. A company might hold an orientation for new employees.

_____ 6. A counselor's main job is to teach swimming.

_____ 7. If Alicia has an aptitude for singing, she is likely to be a good singer.

_____ 8. If you make a commitment to feeding the homeless on Saturdays, you don't have to show up regularly.

_____ 9. Balancing work, school, and family can be a major problem.

_____ 10. After a hurricane, various government and insurance agencies will make an assessment of the damages.

4 The following are comments heard around a college campus. Finish each sentence using the vocabulary words below. Use each word once.

SET ONE

VOCABULARY LIST

declare	faculty	cope	orientation	aptitude

1. "Thanks to my friend Doug's help, I was able to _____ with geometry."
2. "I have decided to _____ my major as art. I am going to fill out the paperwork to-morrow."
3. "I just discovered that I have a(n) _____ for tap dancing!"
4. "I appreciate the _____ on this campus; two of my favorite professors are Remsburg and Ramsey."
5. "I learned about tutoring services at the _____ meeting I came to the week before classes began."

SET TWO

VOCABULARY LIST

counselor	empower	major	assessment	commitment

6. "I will be at the study session tonight. When I make a(n) _____, I stick to it."
7. "I have to go to the _____ office to sign up for a writing test. I want to be placed in the right level of English next semester."
8. "Mr. Diaz is an excellent _____; he told me all about a program the college offers for students who are having problems studying."
9. "I am not sure if I want my _____ to be law or drama."
10. "Next week I become editor of the college newspaper, which will _____ me to make the changes the paper needs."

© 2007 Pearson Education, Inc.

Draw a simple map of your school or college campus. Label the map with at least five vocabulary words showing where you go to do activities at your school. For example, show where you go for *orientation*, where *faculty* offices are located, and where students can visit their *counselors*. You can be imaginative with some of the labels: where you go if you have an *aptitude* for music, where you go to *cope* with writing problems.

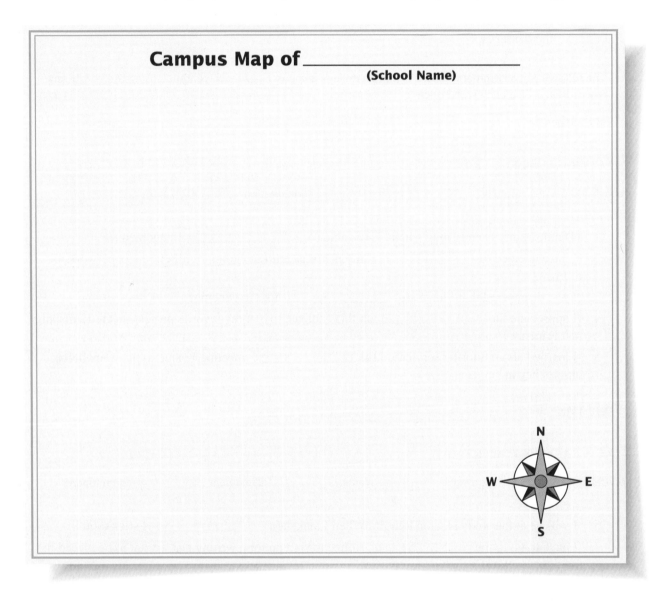

Campus Map of _____
(School Name)

HINT

Campus Resources

Most colleges provide services to improve your educational experience: learn to use these resources. Look into writing centers, computer labs, and tutoring programs to help as you prepare papers or study for tests. If you encounter any problems, consider the benefits of contacting counseling, disabled student services, or the financial aid office. You might also want to check into whether your campus offers a child-care facility. Taking the time to find out where these services are located and what their hours are can make your college experience more satisfying.

▉▊▋ WORD LIST

aptitude [ap′ tə tōōd′]	*n.* 1. talent; ability	**empower** [em pou′ ər, im-]	*v.* to enable; to authorize; to permit
	2. quickness in learning; intelligence	**faculty** [fak′ əl tē]	*n.* 1. teachers at a school, college, or university
assessment [ə ses′ mənt]	*n.* testing; evaluation		2. the ability to do something
commitment [kə mit′ mənt]	*n.* a promise; a pledge	**major** [mā′ jûr]	*n.* the principal area of study chosen by a student in college
cope [kōp]	*v.* to survive; to handle		*adj.* greater in importance; serious
counselor [koun′ sə lûr]	*n.* advisor; person who counsels or gives an opinion on another's actions	**orientation** [ôr′ ē ən tā′ shən]	*n.* program intended to help people adapt to a new environment
declare [di klâr′]	*v.* to announce formally; strongly assert		

▉▊▋ WORDS TO WATCH

Which words would you like to practice with a bit more? Pick 3–5 words to study and list them below. Write the word, its definition, and compose your own sentence using the word correctly. This extra practice could be the final touch to learning a word.

Word	Definition	Your Sentence
1. _____	_____	_____
2. _____	_____	_____
3. _____	_____	_____
4. _____	_____	_____
5. _____	_____	_____

© 2007 Pearson Education, Inc.

3 Planning Your Time

Being Successful

Orientation Handout #6
Planning Your Time

One of the most important lessons a college student can learn is how to deal with time **constraints.** This handout will help you **hone** your time **management** skills. You will become the one in control of your life.

Know your goals: Take the **initiative** and realize that you are responsible for your future. Only
5   you know what you are aiming for. Make a list of the areas in your life that are important to you. Think about what you want to achieve in college, after college, in terms of your health, and for your social life.

Create a to-do list: Make a list of what you need to do to achieve your goals. Create both short-term (weekly) and long-term (semester or longer) lists of what you need to do to achieve each goal.
10   Keep your list current as you complete your goals or change them.

Decide what is important: **Prioritize** your to-do list to decide what you need to do first and what can be done later. Get a weekly planner to schedule important dates (when papers are due or tests are scheduled). Placing items in order of importance will keep you from being **disorganized.** You will find that your life isn't so confusing anymore.

15   Plan your time: Learning how to **allot** your time will help you make wise decisions. Use your planner to write down when your classes meet, times you work, and time for sleep. Then fit in study, exercise, and social time. Knowing how you spend your time will make you more **efficient.**

Don't **procrastinate:** If you put off starting a project by finding other things to do (such as watching repeats on television or throwing socks in a wastebasket), stop and ask yourself why you
20   are afraid to begin. Maybe the job seems too hard. Break the task into smaller parts. It can help to start with the hard part first, and when that part is over, the job won't seem so bad. Set deadlines for yourself and stick to them—that way you can't postpone a job forever. Concentrate on one project at a time, and you will get it done.

Reward yourself: When you finish a project give yourself a reward, even a small one (a slice of
25   your favorite pizza, a CD, an extra thirty minutes on the court). You will be motivated to accomplish more by occasionally rewarding yourself.

Ask for help: Don't be afraid to ask others for help or give them jobs to do if appropriate. You don't have to take care of the kids, cook, and clean alone. You will feel less **frazzled** and have more energy if you ask your family to help with chores. If you aren't sure how to do something, ask for
30   advice. Asking the right person for help can save you hours of wasted time.

By making wise use of your time, you will be able to study, to work, to exercise, and to relax. It takes planning, but setting your goals, writing a to-do list, and deciding on priorities will lead to a more fulfilling life.

© 2007 Pearson Education, Inc.

▌▌▐▌▌ PREDICTING

For each set, write the definition on the line next to the word to which it belongs. If you are unsure, return to the reading on page 20, and underline any context clues you find. After you've made your predictions, check your answers against the Word List on page 25. Place a checkmark in the box next to each word whose definition you missed. These are the words you'll want to study closely.

SET ONE

the first step	to sharpen	to place in order of importance	limitations
the ability to control something			

- ❑ 1. **constraints** (line 2) _____
- ❑ 2. **hone** (line 2) _____
- ❑ 3. **management** (line 2) _____
- ❑ 4. **initiative** (line 4) _____
- ❑ 5. **prioritize** (line 11) _____

SET TWO

tired	well-organized	to give	confused	to postpone

- ❑ 6. **disorganized** (line 13) _____
- ❑ 7. **allot** (line 15) _____
- ❑ 8. **efficient** (line 17) _____
- ❑ 9. **procrastinate** (line 18) _____
- ❑ 10. **frazzled** (line 28) _____

▌▌▐▌▌ SELF-TESTS

1 Match the description with one of the vocabulary words below. Context clues are underlined to help you make the connections. Use each word once.

VOCABULARY LIST

initiative	efficient	prioritize	allot	disorganized
constraints	frazzled	procrastinate	management	hone

1. _____ I will <u>give</u> myself two hours to write a rough draft of my paper; however, I will <u>assign</u> a lot more time to revising it.

2. _____ Because I have lost twenty pounds, I will continue to deal with the <u>restrictions</u> of this diet.

3. _____ Jay <u>puts off</u> doing anything until the last minute.

initiative	efficient	prioritize	allot	disorganized
constraints	frazzled	procrastinate	management	hone

4. _____ Ali took the first step and held a meeting to organize a food drive; we appreciated her getting us started.

5. _____ It's more important to study for my test than watch TV tonight.

6. _____ Isis is so organized that she never forgets any birthdays or anniversaries.

7. _____ I feel tired and stressed.

8. _____ I go to batting practice three times a week to work on my swing.

9. _____ Patricia is so confused that she forgets appointments and loses things.

10. _____ It has taken a while, but I finally feel that I have the ability to control my finances.

2 For each set, finish the analogies. See Completing Analogies on page 5 for instructions and practice.

SET ONE

1. lose : disorganized :: _____   a. hone : knife

2. faculty : student :: _____   b. find : efficient

3. day : night :: _____   c. planner : prioritize

4. dial : a phone :: _____   d. constraint : liberty

5. pencil : write :: _____   e. management : secretary

SET TWO

6. wasteful : careful :: _____   f. disorganized : confused

7. run : a marathon :: _____   g. procrastinate : time

8. gamble : money :: _____   h. allot : forty dollars to spend on shoes

9. drink : thirsty :: _____   i. laziness : initiative

10. job : work :: _____   j. rest : frazzled

3 Finish the want ads from the business section. Use each word once.

VOCABULARY LIST

constraints	disorganized	efficient	frazzled	initiative
allot	management	prioritize	procrastinators	hone

Help Wanted

Looking for a(n) (1)_____ secretary. Applicant must be able to work well with time and budget (2)_____. (3)_____ need not apply—meeting deadlines is essential to our business. If you know how to carefully (4)_____ your time, send your resume to Human Resources, 115 Industrial Rd., Suite B, Hillsdale, 92111.

Help Wanted

If you aren't easily (5)_____, apply to be the head of our Complaints Department. Move into (6)_____ and take control of your career. This is the right place to (7)_____ your people skills. Call (555) 364-2100 today.

Help Wanted

(8)_____ office needs help! If you have the (9)_____ to straighten our files and books, we want you. We need someone to (10)_____ our orders, and get this small operation back on track. Call now (555) 460-3221.

CAREER OPPORTUNITIES

---

4 Circle the correct meaning of each vocabulary word.

1. **hone:** sharpen dull

2. **disorganized:** confused neat

3. **efficient:** messy orderly

4. **frazzled:** exhausted rested

5. **initiative:** first step do nothing

6. **allot:** assign remove

7. **management:** unsure control

8. **prioritize:** random order of importance

9. **procrastinate:** put off get started

10. **constraint:** freedom limitation

© 2007 Pearson Education, Inc.

Write your answers in one or two sentences. Use a vocabulary word in each answer.

Your plan is to move into management. The company will not consider you until you have answered its questionnaire.

HOW ORGANIZED ARE YOU?

1. Which word describes you more—efficient, disorganized, or frazzled? Explain.

   _____

   _____

2. What do you see as the biggest constraint to your doing well in management?

   _____

   _____

3. Describe a situation when you procrastinated or where you took the initiative.

   _____

   _____

4. What skill do you want to hone? Why?

   _____

   _____

5. Do you use a planner to help you allot your time or prioritize your duties? Explain why or why not.

   _____

   _____

HINT

Context Clues

When you encounter a word whose meaning you don't know, keep reading the passage looking for clues to help you decipher the meaning. These clues might be in the same sentence as the unknown word or in a sentence that comes before or after the word. Look for these types of clues in the passage:

Synonyms—words that have a similar meaning to the unknown word
Antonyms—words that mean the opposite of the unknown word
Examples—a list of items that explain the unknown word
General meaning—the meaning of the sentence or passage as a whole that could clarify the meaning of the unknown word

You will not find a context clue every time you encounter a word you don't know, but being aware of context clues will help you determine the meaning of many new words and make reading more enjoyable.

▌▌▌▌ WORD LIST

allot
[ə lot′]
v. to give; to assign

constraint
[kən strānt′]
n. limitation; restriction

disorganized
[dis ôr′ gə nīzd′]
adj. confused; messy; not having order

efficient
[ē fish′ ənt, i fish′ ənt]
adj. effective; well-organized

frazzled
[fraz′ əld]
adj. tired; exhausted

hone
[hōn]
v. to sharpen; to work on
n. a tool for sharpening cutting instruments

initiative
[i nish′ ē ə tiv]
n. the first step; the ability to start a plan

management
[man′ ij mənt]
n. 1. the ability to control something
2. the people who direct a business

prioritize
[prī ôr′ ə tīz′]
v. to place in order of importance

procrastinate
[pro kras′ tə nāt′]
v. to postpone; to put off

▌▌▌▌ WORDS TO WATCH

Which words would you like to practice with a bit more? Pick 3–5 words to study and list them below. Write the word, its definition, and compose your own sentence using the word correctly. This extra practice could be the final touch to learning a word.

Word	Definition	Your Sentence
1. _____	_____	_____
2. _____	_____	_____
3. _____	_____	_____
4. _____	_____	_____
5. _____	_____	_____

© 2007 Pearson Education, Inc.

4 Resume Writing

Presenting the Best You

A **resume** can help you get that important first interview. It should show that you are **compatible** with a company's **philosophy** and that you have the skills to be a good **colleague.**
5 Employers want to hire people who will fit in with their company's values and who get along well with others. The following is an overview of the resume writing process to get you started. Later chapters will go into more detail
10 on each part of the resume.

First, decide whether you are going to write a **chronological** resume or a resume that focuses on your skills. Most people list their work and education history by time, but when
15 you don't have much work history, it can be better to emphasize the skills you have that fit the job. **Consolidate** your information into four basic groups: contact information, job objective, education, and work history.

In your contact information include your 20 name, address, phone number, and e-mail address. In an optional section you may want to add personal information such as professional organizations you belong to that relate to the job and skills that show your aptitude for the 25 position such as foreign languages you speak.

If you make **judicious** use of your time, you can draft a resume in little more than an hour. To start, list your previous jobs. For each job, write the dates you started and ended 30 working there, the name of the company and city and state where it is located, your job title, the duties you performed including equipment or technology you used, skills the job required, and promotions, awards, or other positive 35 experiences involved with the job. Do the same for each of your past jobs. Also list volunteer work if it is **pertinent** to the job. You usually don't need to go back more than ten years, but if you have significant information go back 40 further.

Next list your education from high school on. Write the name of the school, the city and state where it is located, what degree or certificate you earned, courses that relate to 45 your job objective, and awards or other pertinent activities (such as being in student government or an officer in a club). Don't forget **seminars,** workshops, or other types of meetings as learning experiences. 50

Congratulations! You have just finished a basic resume in a short time. Now use a computer to organize the information. Make your resume easy to read, professional looking, and not more than two pages. We won't 55 **belabor** this point, but it is essential that you carefully proofread all of the information to make sure that it is correct and that you haven't misspelled anything. Make copies of your resume on quality paper. Finally, send your 60 resume out and be prepared for those phone calls!

▌▐▐ PREDICTING

For each set, write the definition on the line next to the word to which it belongs. If you are unsure, return to the reading on page 26, and underline any context clues you find. After you've made your predictions, check your answers against the Word List on page 31. Place a checkmark in the box next to each word whose definition you missed. These are the words you'll want to study closely.

SET ONE

| co-worker | a brief document of skills and experiences | well-matched |
| arranged in order of time | values | |

❑   1.   **resume** (line 1) _____

❑   2.   **compatible** (line 3) _____

❑   3.   **philosophy** (line 3) _____

❑   4.   **colleague** (line 4) _____

❑   5.   **chronological** (line 12) _____

SET TWO

| combine | related | overstress | wise | a meeting |

❑   6.   **consolidate** (line 17) _____

❑   7.   **judicious** (line 27) _____

❑   8.   **pertinent** (line 38) _____

❑   9.   **seminar** (line 49) _____

❑ 10.   **belabor** (line 56) _____

▌▐▐ SELF-TESTS

1 Complete the sentences below using the vocabulary words. Use each word once.

VOCABULARY LIST

| philosophy | compatible | colleague | resume | consolidate |
| pertinent | seminar | belabor | judicious | chronological |

1. The _____ on financial planning helped me decide what to do with the money I inherited from my aunt.

2. The lecture last week proved to be quite _____ to today's test. Half of the questions on the test were from the information in that lecture.

3. My _____ and I had a productive meeting. We settled several issues that had been hurting the work environment.

© 2007 Pearson Education, Inc.

philosophy	compatible	colleague	resume	consolidate
pertinent	seminar	belabor	judicious	chronological

4. My friend and I are _____ travelers; we both love to sleep in late.

5. I made a _____ list of my plans for tomorrow: first I will go to class, followed by my dentist appointment, and finally grocery shopping.

6. My _____ is to do my homework as soon as I get home, so I can have free time on the weekend.

7. I tried not to _____ the point, but I wanted to stress that 10:00 p.m. was the latest my son could stay out.

8. The hiring committee was impressed with his _____. He had every skill needed for the job.

9. To make the company run better we are going to _____ three departments.

10. Thanks to the _____ use of club funds throughout the year we have enough money left for a New Year's party.

2 In each group, circle the word that does not have a connection to the other three words. See Chapter 2 for an example.

1.	compatible	friendly	different	well-matched
2.	class	seminar	meeting	book
3.	in order	random	sequential	chronological
4.	resume	summary	poem	work history
5.	wise	stupid	judicious	thoughtful
6.	belabor	overstress	beat	ignore
7.	pertinent	related	unimportant	significant
8.	associate	colleague	stranger	partner
9.	chaos	attitude	belief	philosophy
10.	strengthen	consolidate	divide	unite

3 Put a T for true or F for false next to each statement.

_____ 1. A judge likes to hear information that isn't pertinent to a case.

_____ 2. One can learn a lot by falling asleep at a seminar.

_____ 3. One should try to get along with one's colleagues.

_____ 4. Short stories are rarely written in chronological order.

_____ 5. It is a good idea to check whether a product is compatible with your television before buying it.

_____ 6. A resume should be at least eight pages long.

_____ 7. Parents often belabor a point if it deals with their child's safety.

_____ 8. When traveling it helps to consolidate items to fit them into a suitcase.

_____ 9. Most people would consider playing basketball all afternoon a judicious way to spend their time if they were having a dinner party that night.

_____ 10. Having a philosophy on how to act can help one make important decisions.

4 Complete the resumes below by using the vocabulary words. Use each word once.

RESUME ONE

VOCABULARY LIST

compatible	pertinent	consolidated	colleague	seminars

June 2002–March 2005 Office Manager

Technology Central San Jose, California

Duties: Oversaw 30 employees, gathered (1)_____ information to write annual personnel

reviews, (2)_____ reports from five departments into monthly summary, made sure all new

equipment was (3)_____ with existing equipment, and organized company

(4)_____ on efficiency and working with others. In 2003 and 2004 received Best

(5)_____ award for my diligent work.

RESUME TWO

VOCABULARY LIST

chronological	philosophy	belabor	judicious	resumes

2004 Bachelor's Degree in History, Minor in Business

Superior College Pear Valley, Texas

Pertinent courses: Business History in America, gave a (6)_____ history of American com-

panies from the early colonists to the computer giants; Money and Power, looked at the

(7)_____ of business practices throughout history. My senior seminar paper "A Point to

(8)_____: An Historical Look at How to Solve Conflicts between Management and

Workers" was awarded Best History Composition for the year. Through (9)_____ use of my

time I earned a 3.7 grade point average, worked 20 hours a week in the Career Center tutoring

students on how to write (10)_____, and was in the marching band.

© 2007 Pearson Education, Inc.

Answer the following questions:

1. What kind of seminar would you be interested in attending? _____

2. Use three words to describe yourself as a colleague.

   _____   _____   _____

3. What are two schools you would list on your resume?

   _____

   _____

4. What is a point you would belabor about yourself during an interview? _____

   _____

5. If you were applying for a job overseas, what is one pertinent piece of information you would

   want to include in your resume? _____

6. With what kind of people are you most compatible? _____

   _____

7. What job would you list first if you were writing a chronological resume with your most recent

   job experience first? _____

8. Do you make more judicious use of your time or your money? Explain your choice. _____

   _____

   _____

9. What is your philosophy toward work? _____

   _____

10. What could you consolidate to make your life easier? _____

    _____

HINT

Study Often

Don't try to fit all of your studying into one session before a test. Look at your notes for a class often. Review them the day you write them while the information is fresh in your mind in case you want to add material. Do a weekly review of material so that as you learn new material you can build on the old information. These same ideas apply to learning vocabulary. Look often at the flash cards you make. Even taking ten minutes a day to go over the words for that week will help you remember the meanings. While you are waiting for another class to start, for a friend who is late, or for the bus to come, take some of that time to review the words.

■■■ WORD LIST

belabor
[bi lā′ bər]
v. to overstress; to explain or work at excessively; to beat

chronological
[kron′ ə lo′ ji kəl]
adj. arranged in order of time; sequential

colleague
[käl′ ēg]
v. co-worker; associate; partner

compatible
[kəm pat′ ə bəl]
adj. 1. capable of being in an agreeable situation with others; well-matched
2. capable of efficient operation with other elements

consolidate
[kən sol′ i dāt′]
v. 1. to combine; to unite; to make more compact
2. to make secure or firm; strengthen

judicious
[jōō dish′ əs]
adj. wise; having good judgment; careful

pertinent
[pûr′ tin ənt]
adj. related; important; to the point

philosophy
[fi los′ ə fē]
n. 1. values; beliefs one lives by
2. the study or love of knowledge
3. a calm attitude

resume, résumé, or resumé
[rez′ oo mā′, rez′ oo mā′]
n. a brief document of skills and experiences prepared by a job applicant; a summary

seminar
[sem′ ə när′]
n. a meeting or class for discussion of a specific subject

■■■ WORDS TO WATCH

Which words would you like to practice with a bit more? Pick 3–5 words to study and list them below. Write the word, its definition, and compose your own sentence using the word correctly. This extra practice could be the final touch to learning a word.

Word	Definition	Your Sentence
1. _____	_____	_____
_____	_____	_____
2. _____	_____	_____
_____	_____	_____
3. _____	_____	_____
_____	_____	_____
4. _____	_____	_____
_____	_____	_____
5. _____	_____	_____
_____	_____	_____

© 2007 Pearson Education, Inc.

Look for words with these **prefixes, roots,** and/or **suffixes** as you work through this book. You may have already seen some of them, and you will see others in later chapters. Learning basic word parts can help you figure out the meanings of unfamiliar words.

prefix: a word part added to the beginning of a word that changes the meaning of the root
root: a word's basic part with its essential meaning
suffix: a word part added to the end of a word; indicates the part of speech

WORD PART	MEANING	EXAMPLES AND DEFINITIONS
Prefixes		
dis-	away from, not	*disorganized:* not organized *disappear:* move away from sight
inter-	between, among	*interactive:* making connections between things *international:* between nations or countries
pre-	before	*predict:* to tell in advance *preview:* to see before
Roots		
-chron-	time	*chronological:* following time order *chronic:* all the time
-dic-, -dict-	to say, to tell, to use words	*predict:* to tell in advance *dictation:* the process of saying or reading aloud to be recorded or written by someone else
-man-, -manu-	hand	*manuscript:* a handwritten document *manually:* done by hand
-ten-	to stretch	*intention:* a plan (to stretch toward) *intense:* to an extreme degree (stretched tight)
Suffixes		
-ment (makes a noun)	action, state of being	*assessment:* state of assessing or measuring *merriment:* the state of being merry
-er, -or (makes a noun)	one who	*baker:* a person who bakes *counselor:* a person who counsels or gives advice
-ation, -tion (makes a noun)	condition, act of	*opposition:* the act of opposing or being in conflict *action:* condition of being active or doing

1 Read each definition and choose the appropriate word from the list below. Use each word once. The meaning of the word part is underlined to help you make the connection. Refer to the Word Part list on page 32 if you need help.

VOCABULARY LIST

enchantment	manage	extend	predict	chronological
discourage	intersperse	philosopher	imitation	dictionary

   1. to say <u>before</u> _____

   2. to <u>stretch</u> out _____

   3. to distribute <u>between</u> things _____

   4. to be able to <u>handle</u> _____

   5. relating to <u>time</u> order _____

   6. a person <u>who</u> is wise _____

   7. the <u>state of being</u> charmed _____

   8. a book on how to <u>use words</u> _____

   9. <u>condition</u> of being false _____

 10. to take <u>away</u> one's hope _____

2 Finish the sentences with the meaning of each word part from the list below. Use each meaning once. The word part is underlined to help you make the connection.

VOCABULARY LIST

not	hand	person who	to stretch	before
tells	between	state of being	act of	time

   1. When you go to a <u>pre</u>view of a movie, you see it _____ other people do.

   2. The Olympics is an <u>inter</u>national event. This means it is held _____ different countries.

   3. To have <u>chron</u>ic pain means to have pain all the _____ or constantly.

   4. An act<u>or</u> is a _____ acts.

   5. If someone is feeling merri<u>ment</u>, he or she is in the _____ merry.

   6. When giving a ver<u>dict</u>, the jury _____ the decision it has made.

   7. To set up the <u>tent</u> we had _____ it over the poles.

   8. If you do something <u>manu</u>ally, you do it by _____.

   9. If you <u>dis</u>like someone, you do _____ like him or her.

 10. Gradu<u>ation</u> is the _____ finishing school.

© 2007 Pearson Education, Inc.

3 Finish the story using the word parts below. Use each word part once. Your knowledge of word parts, as well as the context clues, will help you create the correct words. If you do not understand the meaning of a word you have made, check the dictionary for the definition or to see whether the word exists.

WORD PARTS

ation	pre	tend	inter	er
dic	man	chron	dis	ment

THE JOB

June was worried about her (1)_____-
view. She really needed a job. She sat in the waiting
room thinking about her skills. She knew how to
behave in a professional manner. She could speak to
people on the telephone and make them feel like the
company cared about them. She could also

(2)_____tate well—she had no prob-
lem telling other people what to do. She knew she
would be a good office (3)_____ager.

As she waited in the office, she looked at the
other applicants. She could tell one man was very nervous although he was trying to

pre(4)_____ he wasn't. June sympathized with him because she felt the same way. June

went to sit next to him. She told him that she also (5)_____liked looking for a job. Milt

told her that this was not a situ(6)_____ he enjoyed. There was too much to

(7)_____pare for. June asked Milt what time it was. She suggested they

syn(8)_____ize their watches, so they could meet at the coffee shop at the same time af-

ter the interviews. Milt thought that was a great idea as it would ease his resent(9)_____

of having to go through the interview process. They agreed that it was frustrating to be interviewed.

They continued to talk until the interview(10)_____ called June's name.

4 Pick the best definition for each underlined word using your knowledge of word parts. Circle the word part in each of the underlined words.

a. likely to act a certain way

b. state of being satisfied

c. not at the proper time

d. came between

e. to move away from

f. one who translates

g. planned beforehand

h. to say the opposite

i. way of handling things

j. act of expressing joy

_____ 1. The police knew the murder had been <u>premeditated</u> when they found the receipt for the poison dated a week ago.

_____ 2. Her <u>manner</u> was so friendly that I felt relaxed right away at the party.

_____ 3. It was easy to find the <u>anachronism</u> in the picture of the medieval castle: the microwave.

_____ 4. The police told the crowd to <u>disperse</u> because the rally was over.

_____ 5. My boyfriend always <u>contradicts</u> me. Why can't he ever agree with me?

_____ 6. My sister has a <u>tendency</u> to exaggerate; I never know when to believe her.

_____ 7. Mother <u>intervened</u> when the argument between my brother and me got so serious we were about to <u>hit</u> each other.

_____ 8. The <u>translator</u> had a hard job when everyone spoke at the same time.

_____ 9. I appreciated the <u>congratulation</u> cards from my friends when I passed my driver's test—it took me six tries.

_____ 10. My <u>contentment</u> was complete as I nestled under the blanket with a good book and a cup of cocoa.

5 A good way to remember word parts is to pick one word that uses a word part and understand how that word part functions in the word. Then you can apply that meaning to other words that have the same word part. Use the words to help you match the word part to its meaning.

SET ONE

_____ 1. -ten-: intention, contention, extend

_____ 2. -ment: assessment, contentment, resentment

_____ 3. inter-: interactive, international, intervene

_____ 4. -chron-: chronological, chronic, synchronize

_____ 5. -man-, -manu-: manuscript, manually, management

a. action, state of being

b. between, among

c. time

d. hand

e. to stretch

SET TWO

_____ 6. -or, -er: counselor, philosopher, interviewer

_____ 7. pre-: predict, preview, pretend

_____ 8. -dic-, -dict-: predict, dictionary, dictation

_____ 9. -tion, -ation: opposition, graduation, congratulations

_____ 10. dis-: disorganized, discourage, dislike

f. away from, not

g. condition, act of

h. one who

i. before

j. to say, to tell, to use words

© 2007 Pearson Education, Inc.

HINT

Etymologies

An etymology is the history of a word. Some dictionaries will tell in an entry how the word came into existence. There are several ways words are developed, such as being made up, coming from a person's name, or evolving over time from foreign languages. Reading a word's etymology can sometimes help you remember the meaning. For example, the word **addict** comes from the Latin *addictus*, which meant someone given to another as a slave. This history helps to show how being addicted to something is being a slave to it. Not all words have interesting histories, but taking the time to read an etymology can be useful. If you get excited about word origins, there are books available on the subject that show how fascinating words can be.

▌▌▐▌ INTERACTIVE EXERCISE

Use the dictionary to find a word you don't know that uses the word part listed below. Write the meaning of the word part, the word, and the definition. If your dictionary has the etymology (history) of the word, see how the word part relates to the meaning, and write the etymology after the definition.

Word Part	Meaning	Word	Definition and Etymology
EXAMPLE:			
chron-	time	chronograph	an instrument that graphically records time intervals such as the length of an event. Chrono- (time) + -graph (written)
1. pre-			
2. man-			

Word Part	Meaning	Word	Definition and Etymology

3. *dis-* _____

_____

_____

_____

4. *inter-* _____

_____

_____

_____

5. *dict-* _____

_____

_____

_____

▌▐▌▌ WHERE DID IT COME FROM?

Seminar (Chapter 4): comes from the Latin *seminarium* "plant nursery." The word is formed from *semen* "seed" plus *arium* or -ary "pertaining to, connected with." The word seminary also comes from *seminarium.* A seminary is a type of school, such as a secondary school for girls or one for the education of rabbis, ministers, or priests. It also means a place where something is developed. Seminar means "a meeting or class for discussion of a particular subject." The word's origins are connected with the seed of learning.

Incentive (Chapter 8): comes from Latin *incentivus* "setting the tune." The word stem is *incinere* "to strike up or to play." The word is formed from *in-* "in, into" plus *cinere* "to sing" plus *–ivus* or -ive "performing an action." Music obviously played a part in encouraging people. Today an incentive is "something that motivates action or greater effort," and for many people music still fills that role.

© 2007 Pearson Education, Inc.

CHAPTER 6 Odd Places

Journey Beyond the Ordinary

ODD PLACES TOURS

If you are enthusiastic about the unusual, this is the **opportune** moment to travel. Join us for an Odd Places Tour. Enjoy leafing through this brochure and discovering places that excite the
5 imagination. You will also find compatible travel companions on our tours.

Tour 1   Winchester Mystery House   San Jose, California

Departures:
monthly

Sarah Winchester had this house built to **appease** the spirits after inheriting millions of dollars from her husband's interest in the manufacturing of Winchester
10 rifles. Trying to cope with the death of her husband, she went to a psychic who told her that the **malevolent** spirits of those killed by Winchester rifles wanted revenge; however, they couldn't harm her if she bought a house and maintained continuous construction. Mrs.
15 Winchester's grasp of reality must have been a bit **tenuous** at this period because she did as the spiritualist recommended. From 1884 to 1922 for twenty-four hours a day workers built and demolished sections of her house. The result is a house with stairways that end at
20 ceilings, doors that open onto walls, one-inch closets, and other bizarre features. The house at one time had 750 rooms, but many were torn down as the building plans changed daily to soothe the spirits. Join us for an exclusive tour of the house.

Tour 2   The Nazca Lines   Nazca, Peru

Departures:
April 10 and
May 12

These mysterious shapes in the Peruvian desert still 25 **baffle** human understanding. Created about 1,500 years ago, the designs can only be detected from the air. The lines were made using different methods such as moving black pebbles to reveal the white ground underneath or scrapings on rocks. The designs include 30 rectangles, triangles, a giant whale, a monkey, and a spider. Some of the shapes are several miles long. **Interceding** on our behalf, a Peruvian official has arranged for us to fly over figures that few tourists ever see. We have also been lucky to **retain** one of the top 35 experts on the lines. He will help us **speculate** on why the lines were made (as clocks, airfields for the gods, for religious ceremonies). We may even develop new ideas.

Tour 3   Easter Island   Pacific Ocean

Departures:
April 17 and
May 19

With its fantastic statues, Easter Island will be an adventure for all. Most of the huge statues were begun 40 around the year 1100. We will be shown how a dozen islanders could lift a 25-ton statue simply using logs and stones. We will also have **access** to the island's strange wooden tablets, and our guides will provide ideas on what the mysterious writing on the tablets might 45 **symbolize.** One theory is that the shapes do not represent a language, but are memory aids for events in religious celebrations. The unusual thrives on Easter Island—join the journey.

▌▐▐▌ PREDICTING

For each set, write the definition on the line next to the word to which it belongs. If you are unsure, return to the reading on page 38, and underline any context clues you find. After you've made your predictions, check your answers against the Word List on page 43. Place a checkmark in the box next to each word whose definition you missed. These are the words you'll want to study closely.

SET ONE

to confuse	weak	to soothe	favorable	mean

❑ 1. **opportune** (line 2) _____

❑ 2. **appease** (line 7) _____

❑ 3. **malevolent** (line 11) _____

❑ 4. **tenuous** (line 16) _____

❑ 5. **baffle** (line 26) _____

SET TWO

state of being able to approach or enter	to suppose	to hold	to represent
requesting something for someone else			

❑ 6. **interceding** (line 33) _____

❑ 7. **retain** (line 35) _____

❑ 8. **speculate** (line 36) _____

❑ 9. **access** (line 43) _____

❑ 10. **symbolize** (line 46) _____

▌▐▐▌ SELF-TESTS

1 For each set, finish the analogies. See Completing Analogies on page 5 for instructions and practice.

SET ONE

1. doubt : believe ::   _____   a. a writer : composes

2. access : denied ::   _____   b. malevolent : ex-lover

3. baffle : confuse ::   _____   c. laughter : contagious

4. a scientist : speculates ::   _____   d. opportune : inappropriate

5. controlling : boss ::   _____   e. hard : difficult

© 2007 Pearson Education, Inc.

6. calm : appease ::   _____   f. standard : standardize

7. laugh : joke ::   _____   g. sleep : rested

8. symbol : symbolize ::   _____   h. strong : tenuous

9. study : retain ::   _____   i. escort : accompany

10. dark : light ::   _____   j. intercede : argument

2 Finish each sentence using the vocabulary words below. Use each word once.

VOCABULARY LIST

retain	opportune	baffle	tenuous	access
intercede	malevolent	appease	symbolize	speculating

1. I have _____ to my client files on the computer.

2. Let me _____; I speak Italian. They want directions to the Washington Monument.

3. The number of candles on a birthday cake _____ the person's age.

4. The king's control of the country was _____. The people were rebelling, and only the promise of greater freedom could stop them.

5. I was able to _____ the hungry child with a peanut butter and jelly sandwich and a glass of milk.

6. I felt I picked the _____ moment to visit my sister; her family was just sitting down to dessert.

7. I was able to _____ a dozen words of Swedish even after traveling through four other countries.

8. How the murder was committed continued to _____ the police ten years after the crime.

9. Nettie said she was not being _____, but telling my boyfriend that I was at a party with another boy and failing to mention that it was my cousin didn't seem nice to me.

10. My friends and I spent the spring _____ on what the new building downtown was going to be used for. None of us had supposed a fitness center.

3 Circle the correct meaning of each vocabulary word.

1. **baffle:**   frustrate   quiet

2. **intercede:**   to ignore   to request for another

3. **appease:**   excite   calm

4. **access:**   get   stop

5. **malevolent:**   kind   mean

6. **opportune:**   convenient   ill-timed

7. **speculate:**   wonder   know

8. **tenuous:**   slight   powerful

9. **symbolize:**   represent   fake

10. **retain:**   to remember   to forget

4 Finish these headlines from an imaginary travel section. Use each word once.

VOCABULARY LIST

| intercede | access | symbolize | appease | speculate |
| retain | tenuous | baffles | opportune | malevolent |

---

1. **Unexplained Face on Palm Tree _____ Visitors and Scientists in Hawaii**

2. Airlines Attempt to _____ Delayed Passengers with Free Food and Drinks

3. **Online _____ to Health Information While Traveling Improved**

4. _____ Time to Visit Australia: Prices Have Never Been Lower

5. _____ Your Sanity—Escape for a Week to a Greek Island

6. **Tour of Asia's Historic Sites _____ After Virus Spreads in Several Countries**

7. **Mysterious _____ Voice Terrorizes Tourists at Local Hotel**

8. Officials _____ on Behalf of Tour Group Stuck in Border Dispute

9. As Summer Approaches Cities _____ on Becoming Latest Popular Destination

10. **Tourists Amazed by Ancient Cave Painting Believed to _____ a Rocket Ship**

© 2007 Pearson Education, Inc.

LET'S TRAVEL: It's time for a mini-vacation. You have three days and $600 to spend. Decide where you would like to go, and prepare the following items.

1. Select a travel companion. What might this person do that would baffle you on the trip? What could you do to appease the person if there is a problem? _____

_____

2. Imagine a malevolent force (natural or human) that you might encounter on your trip. Who might be able to intercede and help deal with this problem? _____

_____

3. List two places you want access to on your trip. How do these places symbolize your interests?

_____   _____

_____

4. Speculate on what you will do each day. Make a chronological list of activities you want to do. Think about the most opportune time to do each activity. Circle the activity your interest is most tenuous in.

	Day 1	**Day 2**	**Day 3**
morning			
afternoon			
evening			

5. What memories do you think you will retain from this trip?

_____

_____

_____

HINT

Test Anxiety

Studying is essential to do well on a test, but for some people that isn't enough to ease the stress that testing can bring. A few strategies may help you deal with test anxiety. A healthy body leads to a good test-taking experience, so get a good night's rest and eat a healthy breakfast, lunch, or dinner before the exam. Exercise before the exam. Take a walk or do some stretching to help you relax. When you get to the classroom, take a few deep breaths and imagine yourself in a soothing spot such as strolling on a beach or sitting in the shade of a tree. Also picture yourself as being successful on the test; don't focus on any negatives. Being a bit nervous can help during a test by keeping you alert, but too much stress can ruin even the most prepared student's chances of success. If text anxiety becomes a serious problem for you, contact your college's counseling center for advice.

▌▌▐▌ WORD LIST

access
[ak′ ses]

n. state of being able to approach or enter

v. to get

appease
[ə pēz′]

v. 1. to calm; to soothe
2. to satisfy

baffle
[baf′ əl]

v. to confuse; to frustrate

intercede
[in′ tər sēd′]

v. to request something for someone else

malevolent
[mə lev′ ə lənt]

adj. wishing or producing evil or harm on others; mean

opportune
[op′ ər tōōn′]

adj. 1. favorable; appropriate
2. convenient; well-timed

retain
[rē tān′]

v. to hold; to keep; to remember

speculate
[spek′ yə lāt′]

v. to suppose; to wonder; to think curiously about

symbolize
[sim′ bə līz′]

v. to represent; to mean

tenuous
[ten′ yōō əs]

adj. slight; weak; thin

▌▌▐▌ WORDS TO WATCH

Which words would you like to practice with a bit more? Pick 3–5 words to study and list them below. Write the word, its definition, and compose your own sentence using the word correctly. This extra practice could be the final touch to learning a word.

Word	Definition	Your Sentence
1. _____	_____	_____
_____	_____	_____
2. _____	_____	_____
_____	_____	_____
3. _____	_____	_____
_____	_____	_____
4. _____	_____	_____
_____	_____	_____
5. _____	_____	_____
_____	_____	_____

© 2007 Pearson Education, Inc.

Amazing Animals

Special Abilities

Welcome to Animal Chat! Today we are going to explore some **remarkable** animal skills. It isn't **evident** today what attracted the Egyptians to cats, but they believed cats had divine qualities. The penalty for killing a cat was death. Cat temples and graveyards have been discovered in Egypt. Today the **nimble** cat is often seen jumping surprising distances, but it also has an ability that isn't as widely known.

5

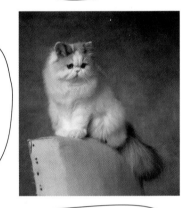

Some cats have demonstrated the ability to find their way back to their owners when lost or left behind. In 1951 Sugar had to be left in Anderson, California, when he wouldn't travel in the car for the family's move to Oklahoma. A neighbor adopted the cat, but within three weeks he disappeared. Thirteen months later Sugar showed up at the Woods' house in Oklahoma. At first Mrs. Woods thought it was another Persian cat that looked like Sugar, but she was able to **verify** that it was Sugar because this cat had the same unusual hipbone deformity as Sugar. It seems **implausible,** but Sugar had traveled 1,500 miles to be reunited with his family.

10

The ways animals communicate are remarkable. A method that baffled humans was how elephants could talk to each other over several miles. The answer proved **elusive** until 1985 when researcher Katherine Payne sensed movement in the air while watching elephants at the zoo. She **surmised** that this movement was related to the fluttering of the elephant's forehead she had just noticed. Using recording equipment, she discovered that the elephants were using low-frequency sounds that humans can't hear. By using this low-frequency sound, which travels well, elephants with their **keen** sense of hearing can warn distant members of the herd about approaching dangers or locate a mate miles away.

15

20

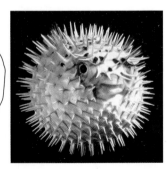

The **tenacious** nature of animals is evident in how they face danger; they don't just give up. To **thwart** an attacker the porcupine fish puffs itself up with water if caught underwater or with air if trapped on the surface. Its spines become erect and can tear the mouth of its attacker. When the danger has passed, the porcupine fish takes a few minutes to let the water or air out and then swims away. Until next time, enjoy the company of our animal friends, and share the planet.

25

For each set, write the definition on the line next to the word to which it belongs. If you are unsure, return to the reading on page 44, and underline any context clues you find. After you've made your predictions, check your answers against the Word List on page 49. Place a checkmark in the box next to each word whose definition you missed. These are the words you'll want to study closely.

SET ONE

clear	causing disbelief	amazing	to confirm
quick and light in movement			

☐ 1. **remarkable** (line 1) _____

☐ 2. **evident** (line 2) _____

☐ 3. **nimble** (line 4) _____

☐ 4. **verify** (line 12) _____

☐ 5. **implausible** (line 13) _____

SET TWO

guessed	to stop	extremely alert or sensitive	tough
hard to get hold of			

☐ 6. **elusive** (line 16) _____

☐ 7. **surmised** (line 18) _____

☐ 8. **keen** (line 22) _____

☐ 9. **tenacious** (line 24) _____

☐ 10. **thwart** (line 25) _____

▌▌▌▌ SELF-TESTS

1 For Set One match each term with its synonym. For Set Two match each term with its antonym.

SYNONYMS

SET ONE

_____ 1. surmise   a. mysterious

_____ 2. evident   b. quick

_____ 3. elusive   c. suspect

_____ 4. nimble   d. unlikely

_____ 5. implausible   e. clear

© 2007 Pearson Education, Inc.

ANTONYMS

_____ 6. remarkable   f. weak

_____ 7. keen   g. dull

_____ 8. thwart   h. common

_____ 9. tenacious   i. allow

_____ 10. verify   j. deny

2 Circle the word that best completes each sentence.

1. It sounded (implausible, nimble), but my daughter assured me that a squirrel had eaten the note from her teacher.

2. The Tennessee state quarter I have been looking for has proved to be quite (elusive, keen).

3. For something printed three hundred years ago, the quality of the book is (implausible, remarkable).

4. His (elusive, keen) mind enabled him to comprehend new duties at work quickly.

5. The storeowner hoped to (verify, thwart) thefts by installing bars on all the windows.

6. Fred was (tenacious, nimble) and finally beat his brother at basketball after losing ten straight games.

7. I want to (verify, surmise) your address, so I can send you a postcard.

8. It's 7:20, and my appointment is at 7:30 twenty miles away. It is (remarkable, evident) that I will not make it there on time.

9. Tricia was excellent at yoga because her body was so (nimble, implausible).

10. I thought I could (surmise, thwart) what my birthday present was after my boyfriend gave me three clues.

3 Answer the questions about each example. Use each word once.

VOCABULARY LIST

verify	elusive	remarkable	evident	implausible
keen	surmise	tenacious	nimble	thwart

1. During her solo, Toni's fingers danced over the piano keys to the delight of the audience. What can be said about her fingers? _____

2. Erik calls the store to confirm that it is open. What does he want to do? _____

3. At four years old, Alexander flew a plane across the country. What would most people call his achievement? _____

4. The windshield was cracked and the bumper smashed. How hard was it for Bob's friends to figure out that he had been in an accident? _____

5. A hamster has avoided being caught for two weeks. What has the hamster proven to be? _____

6. Laura can hear her kids talking three rooms away. What kind of hearing does she have? _____

7. Connie tried to learn the tango, but she kept stumbling during one step. What was that move doing to her? _____

8. Karl, who lives in Los Angeles, said he was late because a herd of elephants was blocking his driveway. What would most people call his reason? _____

9. Marin and Anders were so hungry that they spent most of the afternoon trying to guess what their mom was going to make for dinner. What did the kids spend their time doing? _____

10. Kris refused to quit fishing though he had been out for six hours and hadn't gotten one bite. What word would describe his behavior? _____

4 Complete the following reading by using the vocabulary words. Use each word once.

VOCABULARY LIST

remarkable	evident	verify	thwarts	elusive
implausible	tenacious	surmised	keen	nimble

It is usually (1)_____ that animals have special skills, but some of them aren't so obvious.

For example, it seems (2)_____ that an animal can survive after eating cyanide, but the

golden bamboo lemur does just that. It eats the shoots of a bamboo in Madagascar that contain

cyanide. It eats about 18 pounds a day, which is equal to 12 times the deadly dose for humans.

Scientists have not been able to (3)_____ how the golden bamboo lemur can survive on

such a diet. However, they have (4)_____ different theories. One theory is that eating the

iron-rich soil of the area (5)_____ the ill effects of the cyanide.

Another (6)_____ skill is the way chimps and gorillas have been able to learn American

Sign Language. It was discovered that it was difficult for chimps to form words using speech, but with

their (7)_____ fingers apes have been able to talk to humans. Through the

(8)_____ efforts of researchers, chimps and gorillas have been taught hundreds of words.

Koko, a gorilla, is especially (9)_____. She has learned over one thousand signs. A word

was never (10)_____ for the chimp Lucy. She made up her own words such as "candy drink"

to describe watermelon. Animals certainly have amazed humans with what they are capable of doing.

© 2007 Pearson Education, Inc.

Answer the following questions in the spaces provided.

1. What are two activities you are keen on doing?

_____

_____

2. What animal do you think is especially nimble? _____

_____

3. When have you been tenacious? _____

_____

4. How could you thwart an animal from eating your plants? _____

_____

5. Name a situation where you would need to surmise something. _____

_____

6. How would you verify the statement that chimps can use tools?

_____

_____

7. Create an implausible reason for not doing your homework.

_____

_____

8. What animal do you think is remarkable? Why? _____

_____

9. What is something that has been elusive in your life? _____

_____

10. Name one evident way that animals are important to people.

_____

HINT

Fewer Choices

If you get stuck on one question in a matching or multiple-choice test, go on to the next question. When you finish answering the ones that are easy for you, see which choices are left. With fewer choices the answers should be easier to figure out. Look at Self-Test 1 in this chapter as an example.

▌▐█ WORD LIST

elusive
[i lōō′ siv]
adj. tending to avoid or escape understanding or reach; hard to get hold of; mysterious

evident
[ev′ ə dənt]
adj. easily seen; clear

implausible
[im plô′ zə bəl]
adj. causing disbelief; unlikely; doubtful

keen
[kēn]
adj. 1. extremely alert or sensitive; sharp
2. eager; enthusiastic; intense
3. intelligent

nimble
[nim′ bəl]
adj. 1. quick and light in movement; lively
2. quick to think or comprehend

remarkable
[ri mär′ kə bəl]
adj. great; amazing; uncommon; rare

surmise
[sər mīz′]
v. to guess; to suspect; to assume
n. a suspicion; a theory

tenacious
[tə nā′ shəs]
adj. holding fast; stubborn; tough; firm

thwart
[thwôrt]
v. 1. to prevent; to stop
2. to frustrate

verify
[ver′ ə fī′]
v. to prove the truth of; to confirm

▌▐█ WORDS TO WATCH

Which words would you like to practice with a bit more? Pick 3–5 words to study and list them below. Write the word, its definition, and compose your own sentence using the word correctly. This extra practice could be the final touch to learning a word.

Word	Definition	Your Sentence
1.		
2.		
3.		
4.		
5.		

© 2007 Pearson Education, Inc.

8 Crazy Inventions

Searching for a Buyer

Unusual Inventions

Summer Catalogue

Welcome to our latest issue. We have some great buys for you! We love to **contradict** those who say our items will never be popular. Maybe when they were first invented they didn't do well, but sometimes all it takes is a slight adjustment, or a few years for the public to recognize the beauty in what might seem like a crazy idea. The growth of our company shows that we are doing something right! We certainly aren't an **impartial** source, but we know you will love browsing through our catalogue. A few of our favorites are featured below.   5

Fashion

The "reservoir hat" (page 14) has been a **revelation** for those who travel in hot climates. The hat has a rim that collects rainwater from tropical storms. A carbon strip in the rim helps to remove potentially dangerous matter from the water. When you get thirsty, simply tip your hat and take a sip. Invented in the late 1800s in Germany, the British used this hat during their war with South   10 Africa in the early 1900s with mixed success. Improvements have been made including a removable cup on the top of the hat. We **envision** these hats replacing bottled water. Test this unusual hat on your next trip, and discover its wonders.

If you **loathe** doing laundry on vacation, we have the answer. Invented in the   15 1960s they never quite caught on, but now is the perfect time to bring them back: paper clothes (pages 15–18). We have paper dresses in a variety of colors, paper pants, and even jackets. Wear them once or twice and then throw them away.

Entertainment Time

Are you in a **quandary** about what to   20 get crazy Uncle George for his birthday? Are you looking for a way to amaze your guests? The loop-the-loop bicycle (page 55) is for you. Invented by Karl Lange in 1904 for circus tricks,   25 you can use it in your backyard. You sit on one bicycle and the other bicycle is strapped to your back with the wheels in the air. As you go down the ramp (included in the price) you flip in the air   30 and land upside down on the second bike. Imagine the applause! The bike will go through a careful **inspection** before being shipped to you; our examination helps ensure your safety.   35

Wake Up

Is getting up each morning the most **laborious** task you face each day? We have the answer to your problems. We have two models available (pages 30–32). For those who sleep lighter, we have Samuel S. Applegate's   40 1882 design. When the alarm goes off and you don't move, a pile of cork blocks falls on you. The blocks don't hurt, but they will give you the **incentive** to get up. For those   45 who can continue to sleep under a pile of cork, you need the **ultimate** machine. It tilts your bed and rolls you off if you don't get up when your alarm goes off. Hurry, these   50 machines won't last: there are lots of heavy sleepers out there.

Browse through the catalogue for more fun ideas, and if you get the inspiration to invent something let us know. We are always looking for   55 the unusual.

Note: The catalogue is fictitious, but the inventions are real.

▌▌▌▌ PREDICTING

For each set, write the definition on the line next to the word to which it belongs. If you are unsure, return to the reading on page 50, and underline any context clues you find. After you've made your predictions, check your answers against the Word List on page 55. Place a checkmark in the box next to each word whose definition you missed. These are the words you'll want to study closely.

SET ONE

fair	imagine	to hate	to disagree with	a discovery

- ❑ 1. **contradict** (line 1) _____
- ❑ 2. **impartial** (line 4) _____
- ❑ 3. **revelation** (line 6) _____
- ❑ 4. **envision** (line 12) _____
- ❑ 5. **loathe** (line 15) _____

SET TWO

encouragement	difficult	extreme	a confused state	examination

- ❑ 6. **quandary** (line 20) _____
- ❑ 7. **inspection** (line 33) _____
- ❑ 8. **laborious** (line 36) _____
- ❑ 9. **incentive** (line 45) _____
- ❑ 10. **ultimate** (line 47) _____

▌▌▌▌ SELF-TESTS

1 Circle the correct meaning of each vocabulary word.

1. **contradict:**	to agree	to deny
2. **impartial:**	fair	prejudiced
3. **loathe:**	hate	like
4. **revelation:**	secret	announcement
5. **inspection:**	glance	examination
6. **envision:**	foresee	surprise
7. **laborious:**	lazy	hard-working

© 2007 Pearson Education, Inc.

8. **incentive:**   motivation   obstacle

9. **quandary:**   certain   confused

10. **ultimate:**   secondary   essential

2 Finish the sentences using the vocabulary words. Use each word once.

VOCABULARY LIST

| inspection | contradict | laborious | envision | quandary |
| impartial | ultimate | loathe | incentive | revelation |

1. I was in a _____ about whether to go to my high school reunion or a friend's wedding. Luckily for me, the wedding was postponed.

2. I tried to be _____, but deep inside I really wanted my former high school to win the championship.

3. I _____ getting junk mail.

4. In high school, permission to go to dances was my _____ for doing well on math tests. It worked; I got a "B" in my math class.

5. The _____ revealed that top members of management had been hiding money in a secret account for years.

6. I hate to _____ the instructor, but she said the test would be in two days, which is a Sunday, and we don't have class on Sundays.

7. Doing a research paper seemed _____ to me until I looked at it as a big puzzle.

8. I thought I had test-driven the _____ car until I went to the next dealer and found something even faster.

9. My sister's _____ that she was pregnant surprised all of us.

10. From our phone conversation, I couldn't _____ how my friend had remodeled her kitchen; I had to visit her to see what it looked liked.

3 Put a T for true or F for false next to each statement.

_____ 1. An airplane must go through an inspection before it is allowed to fly.

_____ 2. Winning a free trip for nine friends and yourself is a strong incentive for entering a contest.

_____ 3. Deciding what to major in can be a quandary for some people.

_____ 4. Most people like to be contradicted all the time.

_____ 5. Getting a gold medal in the Olympics is the ultimate goal for some athletes.

_____ 6. Most people would loathe a massage after a hard day at work.

_____ 7. It is easy for most people to envision where they will live and what job they will have thirty years from now.

_____ 8. Most people find relaxing in a lounge chair a laborious task.

_____ 9. It is easy to be impartial about a project one has put hours into doing.

_____ 10. It would be a pleasant revelation if you were notified that a stranger had left you ten thousand dollars.

4 Use the vocabulary words to complete the following analogies. For instructions on how to complete analogies, see Completing Analogies on page 5.

VOCABULARY LIST

inspection	ultimate	envision	impartial	revelation
quandary	incentive	laborious	contradict	loathe

1. mowing the neighbor's lawn : kindness :: what to wear on a big date : _____

2. run : race :: _____ : winning the lottery

3. laugh : a joke :: _____ : 100-degree weather

4. expensive : cheap :: support : _____

5. dancer : nimble :: judge : _____

6. empty : blank :: highest : _____

7. math : subject :: getting $5 for every "A" : _____

8. meeting : seminar :: _____ : discovery

9. rehearsal : play :: _____ : restaurant

10. separate : unite :: _____ : easy

© 2007 Pearson Education, Inc.

Envision yourself ordering from the *Unusual Inventions* catalogue or another catalogue that features products that interest you (for example, clothes, tools, sports equipment). Write two notes to the company. In one explain how much you love the items you ordered and how you consider them the ultimate company to buy from. In the other, tell how much you loathe what you ordered and how dissatisfied you are with their products. Use at least four of the vocabulary words in each note.

NOTE ONE

_____

_____

_____

_____

_____

NOTE TWO

_____

_____

_____

_____

_____

HINT

Make Your Own Tests

A great way to study is to make your own tests in the same style of the tests that you will have in class. Making the tests puts you in the instructor's frame of mind and makes you think about what is important to study.

- Before the first test (or quiz), ask your instructor what format(s) the test will be in—true/false, multiple choice, matching, essay.
- Create a test in the same format(s) with questions that you think will be asked, neatly handwritten or typed.
- Set the test aside for a day.
- The next day, take the test and correct yourself. How much did you remember?
- Make a test for a friend and exchange with each other. Did you come up with similar questions?
- If you examine the first in-class test, you will have a better idea of what the instructor is looking for, and then your homemade tests will be even more useful.

▌▌▌▌ WORD LIST

contradict
[kän′ trə dikt′]

v. to disagree with; to deny; to be in conflict with

envision
[en vizh′ ən]

v. to picture mentally, esp. future events; imagine; foresee

impartial
[im par′ shəl]

adj. fair; unprejudiced

incentive
[in sen′ tiv]

n. encouragement; something that motivates action or greater effort

adj. motivating, as to action

inspection
[in spek′ shən]

n. a close look at; official review; examination

laborious
[lə bôr′ ē əs]

adj. 1. requiring hard work; difficult
2. hard-working; industrious

loathe
[lōTH]

v. to detest; to hate

quandary
[kwon′ drē, -də rē]

n. a confused state; a difficulty

revelation
[rev′ ə lā′ shən]

n. an announcement; a discovery; a surprise or shock

ultimate
[ul′ tə mit]

adj. 1. the most desirable; highest; extreme
2. final; last; essential

n. 1. the finest of its kind
2. the final point or result

▌▌▌▌ WORDS TO WATCH

Which words would you like to practice with a bit more? Pick 3–5 words to study and list them below. Write the word, its definition, and compose your own sentence using the word correctly. This extra practice could be the final touch to learning a word.

Word	Definition	Your Sentence
1. _____	_____	_____
_____	_____	_____
2. _____	_____	_____
_____	_____	_____
3. _____	_____	_____
_____	_____	_____
4. _____	_____	_____
_____	_____	_____
5. _____	_____	_____
_____	_____	_____

© 2007 Pearson Education, Inc.

Focus on Chapters 1–8

The following activities give you a chance to interact some more with the vocabulary words you've been learning. By looking at art, taking tests, answering questions, doing a crossword puzzle, and acting, you will see which words you know well and which you still need to work with.

1. _____

2. _____

3. _____

4. _____

5. _____

6. _____

7. _____

8. _____

9. _____

10. _____

11. _____

12. _____

 **ART**

Match each picture on page 57 to one of the following vocabulary words. Use each word once.

VOCABULARY LIST

intercede	frazzled	disorganized	faculty
tenuous	revelation	loathe	remarkable
consolidate	orientation	compatible	collaborative

SELF-TESTS

1 Pick the word that best completes each sentence.

1. It can be hard for me to make a _____ to exercising, but I do need to make it part of my weekly activities.

    a. constraint   b. faculty   c. commitment   d. seminar

2. Andrea looked _____ after spending all morning working in the hot sun.

    a. frazzled   b. pertinent   c. opportune   d. impartial

3. The meeting was so _____ no one knew what issue they were voting on.

    a. nimble   b. disorganized   c. diligent   d. judicious

4. I want to find a _____ that can lead to a career overseas.

    a. constraint   b. management   c. major   d. synonym

5. It was easy to write a _____ once I got started, and organizing the information about my past jobs and education helped me think about what I want to do with my future.

    a. resume   b. philosophy   c. revelation   d. synonym

6. It was _____ that my nephew was visiting; I saw a pile of toys as soon as I opened the door.

    a. interactive   b. compatible   c. diligent   d. evident

7. Priscilla was so _____ at doing her homework that she could relax on the weekends.

    a. ultimate   b. efficient   c. frazzled   d. pertinent

8. I didn't think the _____ was doing a good job of training the staff; all of the servers were rude and slow.

    a. counselor   b. quandary   c. antonym   d. management

9. Betson's upcoming ten-year high school reunion was the _____ he needed to lose weight.

    a. incentive   b. aptitude   c. theme   d. colleague

10. I want to _____ membership in my gym, so I will continue to pay the dues although I will be gone for over six months.

    a. empower   b. prioritize   c. retain   d. verify

© 2007 Pearson Education, Inc.

2 Finish the story using the vocabulary words below. Use each word once.

VOCABULARY LIST

access	allot	antonyms	context clues	cope
envision	honed	interactive	procrastinated	remarkable

LEARNING WORDS

Matt was afraid to go to college because he did not have a big vocabulary. His friend Dan, however, told him not to be scared because he could take a class to build his vocabulary skills. Matt began to (1)_____ himself in college. At first he pictured himself in Edvard Munch's painting *The Scream,* but after thinking about it overnight, he decided it wouldn't be so bad and he signed up for the class.

On the first day the instructor told the class that the semester would not be difficult if they were willing to study. Matt didn't want to make things hard, so he was ready to (2)_____ several hours a week to doing his assignments. Matt got the book for the class and saw that it was going to be fun to use because it had several (3)_____ exercises. It was great to do activities like art and drama to learn new words. He was going to have to work hard, but he would also enjoy it.

One of the techniques Matt learned first was to look for (4)_____. Those were words around a word that could give him an idea of what the word meant. Matt became an expert at finding these clues. He knew they could come in different forms such as examples, synonyms, or (5)_____. Looking for words that meant the opposite of the word he didn't know was something he had never thought of doing.

On the first quiz Matt got a C. He knew he could have done better if he hadn't (6)_____ and studied only the night before. Matt decided that to (7)_____ with the work he would begin to study his words every day. He now gave at least six hours a week to the class. On the next test and all the rest, Matt got an A.

At the end of the class, Matt had (8)_____ to a lot of new words. He saw his friend Dan one day, who asked how Matt liked the vocabulary class. Matt told him, "I have (9)_____ my reading skills, and I am no longer frazzled by the job of reading college-level books. My vocabulary is now (10)_____, and I can read with confidence." Dan smiled at his friend and nodded in agreement.

Answer the following questions to further test your understanding of the vocabulary words.

1. Who might need help with phonics? _____

   _____

2. What is something you need to take the initiative in? _____

   _____

3. What would the ultimate vacation be for you? _____

   _____

4. What is something that uses chronological order? _____

   _____

5. What can you do to thwart boredom? _____

   _____

6. What is a benefit of being impartial about things? _____

   _____

7. What do you consider the opportune time to study? Why? _____

   _____

8. What do you have an aptitude for? _____

   _____

9. What things in your life should you take a yearly assessment of? _____

   _____

10. When does a person need to make judicious use of his or her time? _____

   _____

© 2007 Pearson Education, Inc.

CROSSWORD PUZZLE

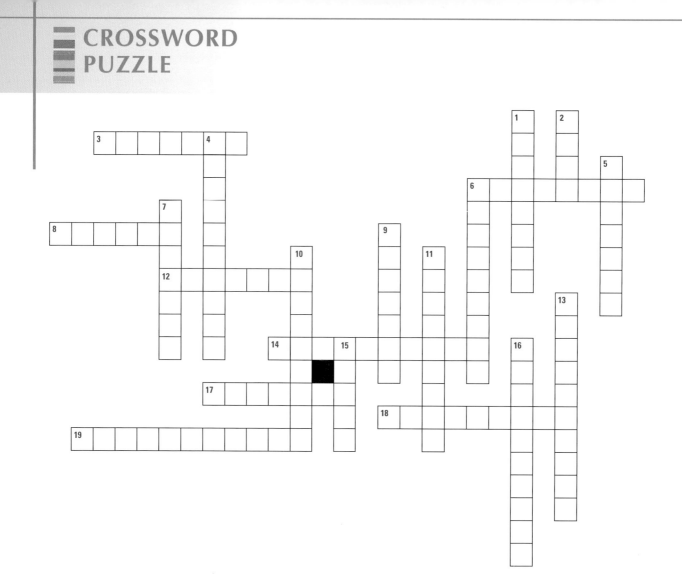

Use the following words to complete the crossword puzzle. Use each word once.

VOCABULARY LIST

analogy	empower
predict	surmise
baffle	implausible
prioritize	symbolize
belabor	keen
quandary	synonyms
constraint	pertinent
seminar	tenacious
contradict	philosophy
speculate	theme

Across

3. to tell before it happens
6. happy, glad, and cheerful
8. can't find your shoes anywhere
12. up : down :: slow : fast
14. I didn't say that!
17. to guess
18. a dog that won't let go of a bone
19. unlikely

Down

1. to go to the ball game or movie
2. Yeah! I can't wait to go!
4. limitation
5. to enable
6. I wonder about that
7. to beat
9. a meeting or class
10. a flag for a nation
11. to the point
13. values; beliefs
15. a focused topic
16. decide what to do first

HINT

HINT

Learn From Your Mistakes

You will be taking quizzes and tests throughout this course, as well as in other classes. Remember that taking a test is simply another way to learn. You learn what you know and what you don't know. When you get a test back, you should always look at your errors, especially if you receive a low grade. It is normal to feel disappointed, but ask yourself first if you really spent enough time with the words before you took the test. If you didn't, then you know what you need to do next time. Then, *look at every error.* If you don't understand why something is wrong, ask the instructor. Go back to the chapter and study all of the exercises where the word was used.

If you follow these procedures, you will learn from the error and will probably not make the same mistake again. Keep in mind that *the grade is always less important than what you learn.* If you really learn how to use the words, you'll get good grades.

COLLABORATIVE ACTIVITY: DRAMA

Charades: You may be given one of the following words to act out in class or you may want to do this activity with a study group. Think about how these words could be demonstrated without speaking. The other people will try to guess what word you are showing.

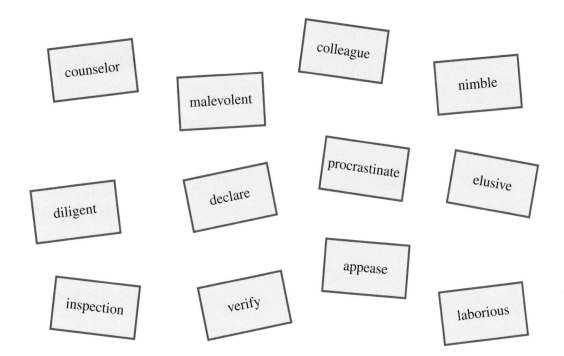

© 2007 Pearson Education, Inc.

10 Music

The Interview*

Music Magazine was lucky to get a rare interview with Louis Armstrong and Ella Fitzgerald. "Satchmo" and the "First Lady of Song" have unquestionably been key people for bringing an **awareness** of jazz music to a broad audience for over forty years. 5

MM: An **appreciation** of jazz has been strong for years, but jazz hasn't stayed the same throughout the years. Louis, what do you think keeps jazz timely?

LOUIS: What **jeopardizes** any kind of music is an un- 10 willingness to change.

MM: Could you **elaborate** on how jazz has changed?

LOUIS: I sang on the streets as a kid, but I was really a **novice** to music when I started to play with King Oliver in New Orleans. As I **associated** 15 with more musicians in Chicago and New York, I learned a lot about jazz. At first there was hot jazz, and the focus of the music was on the group. I was inspired to do more as a soloist, which changed the music scene. Then swing and the big band era prospered. Big bands 20 became less popular in the 1940s, so jazz artists tried new techniques. Bebop, cool jazz, and more developed from there.

MM: Of course, Louis, swing was a style of music you helped to establish. And Ella, you were responsible for finding a place for the voice in bebop. In fact, the **clarity** of your voice is one of the elements that has earned you the title "First Lady of Song." The clearness of your voice is 25 part of what makes you such a great singer, but are you ever sorry you didn't go into dance as you had originally planned?

ELLA: Oh no! When I was 16, I was entered in the Amateur Hour at the Apollo Theater. The dancing of the Edwards Sisters amazed the audience that night. When I went on stage, I just couldn't dance. I changed my talent to singing right then, won first prize, and never regretted my decision. 30

MM: Louis, how about your youth? Some might say your childhood was a bit **maladjusted.**

LOUIS: I had a hard time fitting in. I was brought up in poverty, only went to school through the fifth grade, and got in some trouble with the law. It was music that gave my life meaning.

MM: Ella, were there **preliminary** meetings and lengthy discussions on what you and Louis should record when you made *Ella and Louis Again* in 1956? 35

ELLA: We were really compatible and had a great time working together. It didn't take us long to know what we wanted to do. Louis is a **visionary.** He has an amazing ability to see where music should go; the changes in jazz owe a lot to his work. And he has brought jazz to so many people through his worldwide tours and appearances in 50 films. He even had the ability at 63 to knock the Beatles off the top of the *Billboard* chart with his recording of "Hello Dolly." 40

LOUIS: Enough. All this praise from a woman with 13 Grammy Awards! Working with Ella's humor, beauty, and talent—how could I lose?

*Note: The interview is fictitious.

▌▌▌▌ PREDICTING

For each set, write the definition on the line next to the word to which it belongs. If you are unsure, return to the reading on page 62, and underline any context clues you find. After you've made your predictions, check your answers against the Word List on page 67. Place a checkmark in the box next to each word whose definition you missed. These are the words you'll want to study closely.

SET ONE

a beginner	a favorable opinion	threatens	provide more information	knowledge

❑ 1. **awareness** (line 4) _____

❑ 2. **appreciation** (line 6) _____

❑ 3. **jeopardizes** (line 10) _____

❑ 4. **elaborate** (line 12) _____

❑ 5. **novice** (line 14) _____

SET TWO

unable to conform	connected	introductory	one with an unusual ability to look ahead
clearness			

❑ 6. **associated** (line 15) _____

❑ 7. **clarity** (line 24) _____

❑ 8. **maladjusted** (line 31) _____

❑ 9. **preliminary** (line 34) _____

❑ 10. **visionary** (line 37) _____

▌▌▌▌ SELF-TESTS

1 For each set, match the quotation to the word it best fits. Context clues are underlined to help you make the connections. Use each word once.

SET ONE

VOCABULARY LIST

clarity	novice	visionary	jeopardize	preliminary

1. "At my introductory meeting with the voice instructor, he said I showed great promise." _____

2. "I don't want to risk hurting my fingers before the big piano recital, so I'll skip the football game." _____

3. "I am a beginner at playing the tuba, so I'm not very good yet." _____

© 2007 Pearson Education, Inc.

4. "Her voice is so clear; I can understand every word of her songs." _____

5. "I don't think Ando saw us waving at him. He is probably thinking about some impossible invention he wants to make; he is such a dreamer." _____

SET TWO

VOCABULARY LIST

elaborate	awareness	appreciation	maladjusted	associate

6. "I brought you cookies as a sign of thanks for letting me borrow your notes when I was sick." _____

7. "This party is going to be great. I have every detail thoroughly worked out, from the color of the napkins to the games we will play." _____

8. "I don't fit in my history class. Everyone loves to read dead Romans and debate them, and I can't get excited about them at all." _____

9. "I want to join the garden club so I can meet other people who love plants." _____

10. "I know what is going on, but I don't know how to stop the problem." _____

2 For each set, complete the analogies. See Completing Analogies on page 5 for instructions and practice.

SET ONE

1. whole : entire :: _____   a. unconsciousness : awareness

2. storm : power outage :: _____   b. preliminary interview : talent show

3. plow : farmer :: _____   c. tutoring a friend : appreciation

4. promote : discourage :: _____   d. a dream : visionary

5. vase : flower arrangement :: _____   e. brightness : clarity

SET TWO

6. stay out in the cold : shiver :: _____   f. stable : maladjusted

7. sailor : anchor :: _____   g. bacon and eggs : associated

8. plan : project :: _____   h. drive too fast : jeopardize

9. gloomy : bright :: _____   i. novice : a how-to book

10. jazz : music :: _____   j. elaborate : complicated

3 Circle the word that correctly completes each sentence.

1. The (novice, clarity) of her writing made it easy to understand her argument.

2. I like to invite Colleen to dinner. She has a real (visionary, appreciation) for good food.

3. Dorian (jeopardized, elaborated) his chances of getting into the college he wanted because he forgot to mail his application on time.

4. I consider Willa a (clarity, visionary); things always turn out as she predicts.

5. The (preliminary, maladjusted) plans for the house didn't look a thing like the completed project.

6. My professor says I need to (elaborate, jeopardize) on my ideas for my papers to make a strong point.

7. My (awareness, associate) and I will be at a meeting in Chicago next week.

8. People say Gloria is (maladjusted, visionary), but she is just shy. Once you get to know her she is quite nice.

9. Colin is supposedly a (clarity, novice) at tennis, but he serves like a pro.

10. An (appreciation, awareness) of why I was in the hospital slowly came to me as I remembered the skiing accident.

4 Complete the story below by using the vocabulary words. Use each word once.

VOCABULARY LIST

novice	preliminary	jeopardized	elaborate	visionary
awareness	appreciation	clarity	maladjusted	associated

"I'm so depressed."

"What's wrong Lorna?"

"I just got back from the (1)_____ interviews for the school symphony, and I don't think it went well."

"What happened?"

"The conductor is a (2)_____; he sees the future of music. I so want to be (3)_____ with him. I think I (4)_____ my chances by drooling on him."

"You didn't really drool on him, did you?"

"No, but I kept expressing my (5)_____ for letting me try out and someone had to finally tap me on the shoulder to get me to sit down. I am just a (6)_____ at the cello, so I don't know what I expected. I had (7)_____ plans for my future. I was going to travel the world playing in famous symphonies."

"Well, maybe you can see your world with a little more (8)_____ now. You are an excellent cello player, but your ideas are a little (9)_____ for your current abilities."

"My (10)_____ is hard won now that I have made a fool of myself."

Ring! Ring!

"Hello. Yes. Yes. Yes! Thank you, thank you so much! Goodbye. Maggie, I'm in!"

© 2007 Pearson Education, Inc.

Write a review for a concert you have been to, or pretend you saw Louis Armstrong and/or Ella Fitzgerald in a concert and write a review of the show. Use at least seven of the vocabulary words in your review.

_____

_____

_____

_____

_____

_____

_____

_____

_____

_____

_____

HINT

Getting Ideas

If you feel blocked when starting a writing project, try these prewriting techniques to help you get ideas:

- Freewrite: Write without stopping for five to ten minutes about your topic. Put down any ideas that come to your mind. Here is a time you don't have to worry about spelling, punctuation, or other types of errors—just keep writing.
- Brainstorm: Write your topic at the top of a piece of paper. Then under the heading, list any words or phrases that come to you. Even if an idea sounds silly, put it down; it might lead to your best idea.
- Cluster: Put your topic in the middle of a piece of paper and circle it. Use lines and circles to connect your ideas to the main topic and to put related ideas into groups or clusters. The finished project often looks like a spider web.

▮▮▮ WORD LIST

appreciation
[ə prē′ shē a′ shən]

n. 1. a favorable opinion; recognition of quality
2. feeling of thanks
3. an increase in value

associated
[ə sō′ shē ā təd, -sē ā təd]

adj. connected; joined in some type of relationship

associate
v. [ə sō′ shē āt′, -sē āt]
n. [ə sō′ shē′ it, -sē it]

v. to join; to combine
n. a partner; a companion

awareness
[ə wâr′ nes]

n. consciousness; knowledge

clarity
[klâr′ ə tē]

n. clearness; brightness; easy to understand

elaborate
v. [i lab′ ə rāt′]
adj. [i lab′ ər it]

v. 1. provide more information
2. to work out thoroughly
adj. planned with attention to details; complicated

jeopardize
[jep′ ûr dīz′]

v. to risk; to threaten

maladjusted
[mal′ ə jus′ tid]

adj. 1. unable to conform
2. emotionally unstable
3. not well fitted

novice
[nov′ əs]

n. a beginner

preliminary
[pre lim′ ə när′ ē]

adj. beginning; introductory

visionary
[vizh′ ən er′ ē]

n. 1. one with an unusual ability to look ahead; a prophet
2. one given to impractical ideas; a dreamer
adj. not currently possible

▮▮▮ WORDS TO WATCH

Which words would you like to practice with a bit more? Pick 3–5 words to study and list them below. Write the word, its definition, and compose your own sentence using the word correctly. This extra practice could be the final touch to learning a word.

Word	Definition	Your Sentence
1. _____	_____	_____
_____		
2. _____	_____	_____
_____		
3. _____	_____	_____
_____		
4. _____	_____	_____
_____		
5. _____	_____	_____
_____		

© 2007 Pearson Education, Inc.

A Fun Read

The Times

Elaine ON BOOKS

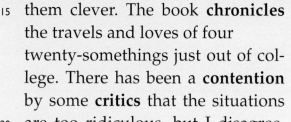

A *Holiday for Four* is a holiday for reading. If you think reading is a **burden**, this is a book that will make you reconsider your opinion. The writing is witty and the characters are loads of fun. The **predicaments** the characters get into are surprising and the ways they get out of

Reviewed by
Elaine Lewis

them clever. The book **chronicles** the travels and loves of four twenty-somethings just out of college. There has been a **contention** by some **critics** that the situations are too ridiculous, but I disagree.

There is **sufficient** development of the characters' personalities to believe that they could get themselves into such humorous fixes as getting locked in a castle when they get lost while on a tour. Nothing is **superfluous** in the novel. All the characters and settings are vital to creating this lively tale. If your life is getting **monotonous**, take a break and read Adele Oslong's *A Holiday for Four*. It is **fiction** at its best! I can't wait for her next **manuscript** to reach the publisher.

▌▐ █▌ PREDICTING

For each set, write the definition on the line next to the word to which it belongs. If you are unsure, return to the reading on page 68, and underline any context clues you find. After you've made your predictions, check your answers against the Word List on page 73. Place a checkmark in the box next to each word whose definition you missed. These are the words you'll want to study closely.

SET ONE

an argument	a difficult job	a person who expresses opinions	records
difficult or ridiculous situations			

❏ 1. **burden** (line 6) _____

❏ 2. **predicaments** (line 11) _____

❏ 3. **chronicles** (line 15) _____

❏ 4. **contention** (line 18) _____

❏ 5. **critic** (line 19) _____

SET TWO

a document	enough	an invented story	more than is needed	boring

❏ 6. **sufficient** (line 21) _____

❏ 7. **superfluous** (line 29) _____

❏ 8. **monotonous** (line 34) _____

❏ 9. **fiction** (line 36) _____

❏ 10. **manuscript** (line 37) _____

▌▐ █▌ SELF-TESTS

1 Complete the sentences using the vocabulary words below. Use each word once.

VOCABULARY LIST

burdened	critics	monotonous	manuscript	chronicles
contention	fiction	sufficient	predicament	superfluous

1. _____ comment on the sets in a play, as well as the plot and acting.
2. All the sentences are the same pattern, and the writer keeps using the same words over and over. I don't want to read another word of this _____ book.
3. I was in _____ to win the race until I tripped and broke my nose.
4. The author's _____ was turned down two hundred times before it was published.

© 2007 Pearson Education, Inc.

5. I bought a clock and most of the packaging was _____. It didn't need to be wrapped in five layers.

6. My English professor has _____ me by assigning an entire novel to read and three essays to write in the next two weeks.

7. This book _____ how the Roman Empire fell apart.

8. My _____ is how to get to class now that my car won't start.

9. I have _____ time to write my paper if I start today.

10. I could tell your story about sitting inside all day studying was _____. Hide the sweaty t-shirt and fast-food containers next time to make it believable.

2 Use the vocabulary words to complete the analogies. See Completing Analogies on page 5 for instructions and practice. Use each word once.

VOCABULARY LIST

burden	monotonous	sufficient	contention	predicament
chronicles	critic	manuscript	superfluous	fiction

1. true : false :: fact : _____

2. upset : worried :: enough : _____

3. song : composer :: review : _____

4. sculptor : statue :: writer : _____

5. war : peace :: harmony : _____

6. slow : fast :: lighten : _____

7. zebra : animal :: one's head stuck in a fence : _____

8. rain : picnic cancelled :: historical events : _____

9. small : little :: extra : _____

10. boring : stimulating :: exciting : _____

3 Match the vocabulary word to its synonym.

_____ 1. contention   a. document

_____ 2. burden   b. difficulty

_____ 3. monotonous   c. unnecessary

_____ 4. sufficient   d. record

_____ 5. fiction   e. reviewer

_____ 6. predicament   f. argument

_____ 7. critic   g. dull

_____ 8. chronicle   h. load

_____ 9. manuscript   i. enough

_____ 10. superfluous   j. untrue

4 Finish the reviews from the backs of fictitious books. Use each word once.

VOCABULARY LIST

monotonous	fiction	chronicles	sufficient	manuscript
burdened	superfluous	contention	critics	predicaments

1. "Rosenquist's first _____ is a gem! This is a writer who will go far." —*Charleston Sun*

2. "Nothing _____ in a Dicken's novel! Every character—all twenty—are needed to keep this tangled tale going." —*The London Gazette*

3. "A must read! As embarrassing as Penelope's _____ are, she keeps going until she solves the case. . . . She is a detective I want to meet." —*The Village Rag*

4. "There isn't _____ room in this column to sing the praises of *The Apartment Next Door*. . . . Why did the novel have to end?" —*The Norman Times*

5. "Derby McDermish has lived in the same house for fifty years, he has the same breakfast, lunch, and dinner every day, and he owns two pairs of pants—both brown. Only Austen could make such a _____ character funny. . . . Cheers for Austen and McDermish!" —*The Kirkland Star*

6. "Where does fact end and _____ begin in Jackson's novel about the sinking of the *Lusitania*? Something to ponder. . . . worth reading." —*The Yearly News*

7. "Emma Garcia feels _____ with four kids, an unemployed husband, a nosey mother, and a boss who expects perfection. And then she meets a stranger. . . . An engrossing look into one woman's personal journey." —*Brownsville Examiner*

8. "*The Invasion* _____ examines attacks and attackers from the Vikings to Vietnam. A must read for any fan of history." —*History Alive*

9. "The _____ agree that Stevenson knows what he's doing. Every novel outdoes the last! Enjoy!" —*Monterey Mirror*

10. "A collection of short stories this good is rare. *Ripening* will certainly be in _____ for some notable awards this year. . . . remarkable work. . . . " —*Binghamton Press*

© 2007 Pearson Education, Inc.

Answer the following questions:

1. Name a burden in your life. _____

2. Name something that has been a point of contention between you and a friend.

   _____

3. What field of art or entertainment would you like to be a critic for? Why? _____

   _____

4. What is one of your favorite works of fiction? _____

5. Name something that you find monotonous. _____

6. Name a predicament you have been involved in. _____

7. What historical event would you like to chronicle? _____

8. What is something one needs sufficient time to do? _____

9. What would you like to write a manuscript about? _____

10. Think of a gathering you have attended. What items were superfluous? _____

    _____

HINT

Creating a Study Group

A class can be more rewarding if you find classmates to study with. To create effective study groups, keep these points in mind.

- Get people who really want to learn, not just socialize.
- Have everyone who is interested in the group write out a weekly schedule with class times, work schedules, family obligations, and the best times to meet. Exchange e-mail addresses and phone numbers so you can easily contact each other.
- Pick a time that can accommodate most people; it may be impossible to get everyone together all the time.
- Decide how often you will meet—once a week, every other week, once a month.
- Find a place to meet. See whether the library has study group rooms or meet at a person's house where you can snack, but where you won't be interrupted by the telephone, children, or other distractions.

▮▮▮▮ WORD LIST

burden
[bûr′ dən]

   n. a difficult job, task, or load to carry

   v. to load or overload; to keep down

chronicle
[kron′ i kəl]

   v. to record

   n. a chronological record of historical events

contention
[kən ten′ shən]

   n. 1. an argument
      2. a striving to win in competition

critic
[krit′ ik]

   n. a person who expresses opinions, good or bad, especially about the arts (for example, books, movies, art, music)

fiction
[fik′ shən]

   n. an invented story; not factual or true

manuscript
[man′ yoo skript]

   n. a document, generally handwritten

monotonous
[mə not′ ən əs]

   adj. having no variety; boring

predicament
[pri dik′ ə mənt]

   n. a difficult, embarrassing, or ridiculous situation

sufficient
[sə fish′ ənt]

   adj. enough

superfluous
[soo pûr′ floo əs]

   adj. more than is needed; excessive

▮▮▮▮ WORDS TO WATCH

Which words would you like to practice with a bit more? Pick 3–5 words to study and list them below. Write the word, its definition, and compose your own sentence using the word correctly. This extra practice could be the final touch to learning a word.

Word	Definition	Your Sentence
1.		
2.		
3.		
4.		
5.		

© 2007 Pearson Education, Inc.

Winners and Losers

PARTY TIME!

In preparation for my yearly movie party, I have created the following questionnaire. There is always a lot of **hype** about movies that are up for awards. It is time to forget all the ads you have seen on television and the articles on the Internet and think about *your* favorite and least favorite movies of all time. We will **bestow** our own awards at the party. I'll have ballots ready for the voting.

What kind of movie **buff** are you? What types of movies get you excited: westerns, romances, action? (I find it is a good idea to know what people like before I say something to insult their favorite kind of film.)

_____

_____

What traits most **nettle** you when watching a movie? Does it annoy you when actors talk too fast, when every scene is shot in shadows, if loose ends aren't tied up? List your gripes and the films that inspire them.

_____

_____

Who is the most **villainous** movie character? When you are thinking of evil characters, remember they can come in many forms: the shark in Jaws, The Wicked Witch of the West, or the computer Hal.

_____

_____

Pick you own **superlative** and **category** for us to vote on (examples: the scariest movie, funniest scene, or most spectacular setting).

_____

_____

_____

What has been the biggest movie **blunder**? (Is there an actor you think should never have been given a part, or a disastrous remake of a classic film, or some other kind of mistake we can't let the film world forget?)

_____

_____

I am certain your answers will **generate** some heated discussions! Bring your completed questionnaire to the party and **qualify** for a chance to win two DVDs courtesy of me.

See you March 5th at 6 p.m.!
As always there will be great films,
excellent appetizers, and delicious drinks!

For each set, write the definition on the line next to the word to which it belongs. If you are unsure, return to the reading on page 74, and underline any context clues you find. After you've made your predictions, check your answers against the Word List on page 79. Place a checkmark in the box next to each word whose definition you missed. These are the words you'll want to study closely.

SET ONE

present	an admirer	excess promotion	a mistake	evil

❑ 1. **hype** (line 3) _____

❑ 2. **bestow** (line 6) _____

❑ 3. **buff** (line 7) _____

❑ 4. **villainous** (line 14) _____

❑ 5. **blunder** (line 24) _____

SET TWO

to start up	to irritate	a class, group, or division	to meet the requirements
an exaggerated expression			

❑ 6. **nettle** (line 31) _____

❑ 7. **superlative** (line 38) _____

❑ 8. **category** (line 39) _____

❑ 9. **generate** (line 47) _____

❑ 10. **qualify** (line 50) _____

▌▌▐▌▌ SELF-TESTS

1 Circle the correct meaning of each word.

1. **hype:**   ignore   go on about

2. **villainous:**   behave badly   do good

3. **blunder:**   perfect   make a mistake

4. **generate:**   create   finish

5. **bestow:**   give   withdraw

6. **category:**   a logical group   doesn't fit

7. **qualify:**   has the skill   hasn't a clue

© 2007 Pearson Education, Inc.

8. **nettle:**   irritate   delight

9. **buff:**   excited about   couldn't care less

10. **superlative:**   greatest   nice enough

2 Finish the following story using the vocabulary words. Use each word once.

VOCABULARY LIST

villainous	superlatives	category	generate	blunders
buffs	bestows	hype	nettled	qualify

Claire and Diana decide to go to the movies on Saturday night. As they approach the multiplex, finishing their sodas from the James Bond cups they got at the fast food restaurant, they notice another huge billboard for the new Bond movie. They are so tired of the (1)_____ for this film. Claire and Diana won't be seeing the Bond film because they are romance (2)_____. They can't wait to see the picture about a woman who finds love while traveling in South America.

They sit down just in time for the beginning. From a distance, the camera shows a boat slowly sailing down the Amazon at sunset. Then the camera comes in closer to reveal a blond woman in a white evening dress, boa, and a huge jewel-studded necklace walking toward one of the cabins. A man approaches, and (3)_____ a beautifully wrapped box into her hands. She smiles, enters a cabin, and closes the door behind her.

A dark-haired woman exits the cabin moments later with an evil look in her eye. She is holding a gun and a large emerald. She quickly puts both of them in a bag. She signals to a small boat close by and disappears in it. Someone yells, "Murder!" It is clear to Claire and Diana that she is a (4)_____ character.

Sandra Bullet, a private detective, rushes out of her cabin. At the same time, two doors down, Antonio Dashing thrusts open his door. Claire whispers to Diana, "These two certainly belong in the good-looking (5)_____."

Sandra and Antonio meet at the murdered woman's door. Antonio stares appreciatively at Sandra, but stops her from entering. "I'm with the Secret Service, and I don't want any (6)_____ made here," he tells her.

Sandra explains, "I'm a detective; I (7)_____ for this job. I'm good—very good—at what I do."

Antonio looks at her and nods, "I'm sure you are. Please join me in solving this case."

Diana whispers, "This relationship is going to (8)_____ some heat." Claire nods.

As the movie progresses, Sandra and Antonio collaborate to find the missing emerald of the Incas and end up falling in love. When the movie is over, Claire gushes, "That was the greatest love story I have ever seen. There are so many (9)_____ I could use to describe this film." Diana, on the other hand, declares, "Give me a break! It was easy to tell where they were going to find the jewel, how they were going to get it back, and when they were going to go to bed. But what really (10)_____ me was the silly dialogue throughout the film—no one talks like that!"

3 Put a T for true or F for false next to each statement.

_____ 1. Traveling for miles to go to a film festival every weekend would be a sign that one is a movie buff.

_____ 2. Placing a full-page ad in the local paper for a new movie is an example of hype.

_____ 3. People don't need to qualify for the Olympics; anyone can show up and compete.

_____ 4. Getting a perfect score on a test is usually considered a blunder.

_____ 5. It can help to talk to other people to generate ideas about a topic.

_____ 6. "The best issue ever" is a superlative statement.

_____ 7. Baking cookies to share with co-workers would be considered villainous by most people.

_____ 8. It nettles most people when others are polite.

_____ 9. Music stores are rarely organized by categories like jazz, pop, and country.

_____ 10. A city might bestow an honor on a person who rescued a drowning child.

4 Complete the sentences using the vocabulary words below. Use each word once.

VOCABULARY LIST

qualify	buff	hype	nettle	generate
categories	bestow	blunder	villainous	superlatives

1. A mascot's job is to _____ excitement in the crowd.
2. Primo was flattered when the company decided to _____ its "hardest worker of the year" award on him.
3. Kidnapping is considered a _____ action.
4. A person usually needs to _____ to be on a swim team.
5. Forgetting to bring one's homework to class would be a _____.
6. Verda is a music _____; she goes to concerts five nights a week.
7. Romance, mystery, and science fiction are examples of _____ one would find in a bookstore.
8. The company really tried to _____ the movie with billboards all over town, constant ads on television, and toys at fast-food chains.
9. Apolo raved about my cooking: "Fantastic! Magnificent! The best pasta I have ever had." I appreciated the _____ even if I wasn't sure they were true.
10. Slow cars in the fast lane can really _____ some drivers.

© 2007 Pearson Education, Inc.

Generate two responses for each of the following:

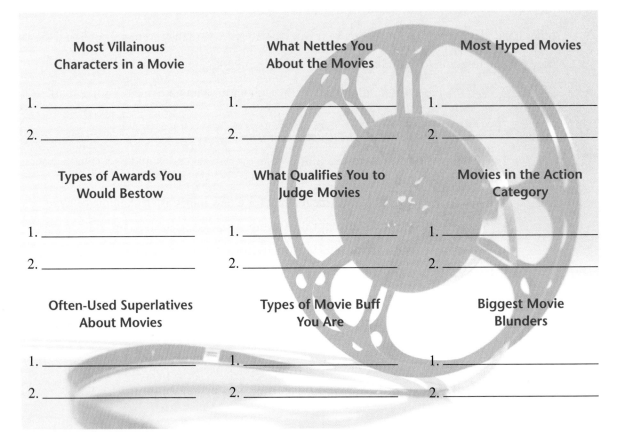

Most Villainous
Characters in a Movie

1. _____

2. _____

What Nettles You
About the Movies

1. _____

2. _____

Most Hyped Movies

1. _____

2. _____

Types of Awards You
Would Bestow

1. _____

2. _____

What Qualifies You to
Judge Movies

1. _____

2. _____

Movies in the Action
Category

1. _____

2. _____

Often-Used Superlatives
About Movies

1. _____

2. _____

Types of Movie Buff
You Are

1. _____

2. _____

Biggest Movie
Blunders

1. _____

2. _____

HINT

Meeting with a Study Group

For an efficient study group, keep these points in mind when you get together:

- Pick a place to meet that is conducive to studying. See whether the library has study group rooms. You want a place where you can talk freely and where you won't be interrupted by telephones, children, or other disturbances.
- Bring the necessary books, notes, and other materials to each session.
- Ask various group members to be "the expert" on different chapters or areas of study—have them share their in-depth study with the other group members.
- Give everyone a chance to participate, respect each person's views, and discover each person's strengths.
- Assign someone to keep the group on track and to be aware of time limits. Gently remind people who get off topic that you are all there to study. Ask anyone to leave who does not really want to study.
- Evaluate how useful the session was and decide what changes may be needed for the next time. Try to make the study sessions fun and productive.

▌▌▌▌ WORD LIST

bestow
[bi stō′]
v. to give; to confer; to present

hype
[hīp]
n. excess promotion

blunder
[blun′ dûr]
n. a mistake
v. to make a mistake

nettle
[net′ əl]
v. to irritate; to annoy

buff
[buf]
n. an admirer; a follower

qualify
[kwäl′ ə fī′]
v. to meet the requirements

category
[kat′ ə gôr′ ē]
n. a class, group, or division

superlative
[soo pûr′ lə tiv]
n. an exaggerated expression, usually of praise

generate
[jen′ ə rāt′]
v. to start up; to develop; to create

villainous
[vil′ ə nəs]
adj. evil; very wicked

▌▌▌▌ WORDS TO WATCH

Which words would you like to practice with a bit more? Pick 3–5 words to study and list them below. Write the word, its definition, and compose your own sentence using the word correctly. This extra practice could be the final touch to learning a word.

Word	Definition	Your Sentence
1.		
2.		
3.		
4.		
5.		

© 2007 Pearson Education, Inc.

13 Word Parts II

Look for words with these **prefixes**, **roots**, and/or **suffixes** as you work through this book. You may have already seen some of them, and you will see others in later chapters. Learning basic word parts can help you figure out the meanings of unfamiliar words.

prefix: a word part added to the beginning of a word that changes the meaning of the root
root: a word's basic part with its essential meaning
suffix: a word part added to the end of a word; indicates the part of speech

WORD PART	MEANING	EXAMPLES AND DEFINITIONS
Prefixes		
il-, im-, in-, ir-	in, into, on	*impress:* have an impact on *intention:* plan to do
il-, im-, in-, ir-	not	*immovable:* not able to move; set *invincible:* not able to be hurt
mal-	bad, wrong, ill	*malicious:* wanting to do wrong; full of malice *malfunction:* working badly
Roots		
-clar-	clear	*clarify:* to make a point clear *declare:* to state clearly
-gen-	birth, creation	*generate:* to create something *generous:* willing to give or share
-lab-	work	*collaborative:* working together *laboratory:* a workshop for scientific experiments
-scrib-, -script-	write	*scribble:* to write quickly *manuscript:* a handwritten document
Suffixes		
-able, -ible (makes an adjective)	capable of	*remarkable:* capable of being noticed *possible:* capable of being done
-ive (makes an adjective)	performing an action	*interactive:* the action of making connections *decorative:* the action of decorating or looking nice
-ness (makes a noun)	state of being	*awareness:* the state of being aware or knowing *sadness:* the state of being sad or unhappy

1 Read each definition and choose the appropriate word. Use each word once. The meaning of the word part is underlined to help you make the connection. Refer to the Word Parts list if you need help.

VOCABULARY LIST

productive	manuscript	malnourished	collaborate	courageousness
inspect	illogical	clarify	generate	invincible

1. the <u>action</u> of making something _____
2. the <u>state of being</u> brave _____
3. to look <u>into</u> something _____
4. <u>to create</u> something _____
5. suffering from <u>bad</u> nutrition _____
6. <u>not</u> capable of being hurt _____
7. to make <u>clear</u> _____
8. <u>not</u> logical _____
9. <u>work together</u> _____
10. a <u>written</u> document _____

2 Finish the sentences with the meaning of each word part. Use each meaning once. The word part is underlined to help you make the connection.

VOCABULARY LIST

clear	workers	creation	write	capable of
bad	not	into	state of being	performing an action

1. Labor Day honors _____.
2. My <u>in</u>tention was to become a lawyer. I wanted to go _____ law to help others.
3. The plan was <u>ir</u>regular because we usually meet at one o'clock and _____ at two.
4. It is impossib<u>le</u> for me to attend the meeting at 6 a.m.; I am not _____ getting up that early.
5. When something <u>mal</u>functions, it goes _____.
6. The _____ sad is called sad<u>ness</u>.
7. Her <u>gener</u>ous nature led to the _____ of the fund to help students buy books.
8. He <u>scrib</u>bled the note on the back of an envelope. He would later _____ it on a piece of paper.
9. The candidate <u>de</u>clared he was going to run for office; he made his position _____ to everyone.
10. The decora<u>tive</u> hanging is _____ of making the room more cheerful.

© 2007 Pearson Education, Inc.

3 Finish the story using the word parts below. Use each word part once. Your knowledge of word parts, as well as the context clues, will help you create the correct words. If you do not understand the meaning of a word you have made, check the dictionary for the definition or to see whether the word exists.

WORD PARTS

in	clar	able	ive	mal
lab	gen	scribe	im	ness

THE HAPPY HORROR

I don't know how to de⁽¹⁾_____ the night I had last night. I awoke when I heard a strange noise. At first I thought it was the wind, but that idea turned out to be ⁽²⁾_____accurate. It was something more ⁽³⁾_____evolent, or so I thought at first. It was my great-grandfather's ghost. He had been a ⁽⁴⁾_____orer; he worked in the fields of our old farm. I had been studying my family's ⁽⁵⁾_____ealogy, and I had come across a picture of him in a scrapbook. He was a very ⁽⁶⁾_____pressive man. He was tall and had an angry face. With much firm⁽⁷⁾_____ I asked him what he wanted with me. He told me he had come back for "a special reason." I asked for some ⁽⁸⁾_____ification of that statement. He told me that he found me to be an admir⁽⁹⁾_____ person and that I was the only member of the family he could trust. He said I wouldn't find what I had to do offens⁽¹⁰⁾_____; he said I would likely enjoy it. After digging in the backyard for an hour, I found the thousand dollars he had hid, and he disappeared when I smiled at him.

4 Pick the best definition for each underlined word using your knowledge of word parts. Circle the word part in each of the underlined words.

a. capable of being true

b. ill smelling

c. a coming in

d. hard to find

e. not capable of being trusted

f. state of having warm feelings

g. a formal statement

h. taking long, hard work

i. the creation of something

j. a message at the end of a letter

_____ 1. My <u>fondness</u> for my aunt goes back to my childhood when she took me to the park to play.

_____ 2. The *Declaration of Independence* clearly stated the views of the American colonies toward England.

_____ 3. The <u>genesis</u> of the idea for Sarah's surprise party came from Sarah herself.

_____ 4. It is <u>probable</u> that I will be late to the meeting because I am coming from across town, and the traffic is bad at noon.

_____ 5. The babysitter's actions were <u>irresponsible</u>—how could she leave a baby alone in a bathtub?

_____ 6. The <u>malodorous</u> air of the basement caused me to step back before entering.

_____ 7. There was an <u>influx</u> of students to the college when the school began to offer more literature courses; students had wanted to read more.

_____ 8. When I tried to find my friend to get the money he owed me, he was very <u>elusive</u>.

_____ 9. It wasn't until the <u>postscript</u> that John wrote what time he would arrive.

_____ 10. Making the garage sparkle was a <u>laborious</u> task.

5 A good way to remember word parts is to pick one word that uses a word part and understand how that word part functions in the word. Then you can apply that meaning to other words that have the same word part. Use the words to help you match the word part to its meaning.

SET ONE

_____ 1. -clar-: clarify, clarity, declare

_____ 2. -ive: interactive, supportive, decorative

_____ 3. il-, im-, in-, ir-: illiterate, impartial, invincible

_____ 4. -lab-: collaborative, elaborate, laboratory

_____ 5. mal-: maladjusted, malicious, malfunction

a. work

b. bad, wrong, ill

c. clear

d. not

e. performing an action

SET TWO

_____ 6. -ness: awareness, tenderness, happiness

_____ 7. -gen-: generate, generous, congenial

_____ 8. -able, -ible: remarkable, possible, probable

_____ 9. il-, im-, in-, ir-: influx, inspect, immerse

_____ 10. -scrib-, script- : scribble, inscribe, manuscript

a. capable of

b. in, into, on

c. write

d. birth, creation

e. state of being

© 2007 Pearson Education, Inc.

HINT

Read for Fun

Many people forget that reading for fun makes a better reader overall. If you think you don't like to read, search for reading material about subjects that interest you. Textbooks are not always the most exciting reading material, so don't give up on reading if you don't enjoy what you currently have to read.

Evaluate your interests to see what kind of material you might like to read:

- Do you like to keep up on current events? Become a newspaper or weekly newsmagazine reader.
- Do you have a hobby? Subscribe to a magazine on the topic.
- Do you like to look into people's lives? Pick up a collection of short stories or a novel. You can find everything from romance to mystery in fiction writing.
- Is there a time period you are interested in? Nonfiction and fiction books deal with events from ancient Egypt to the unknown future.
- Are you interested in travel or different countries? Try books by authors from foreign lands.
- Do you like to read in short spurts or for long periods? Newspaper articles, essays, poetry, and short stories may appeal more to those who like to read a little at a time. Novels, plays, and nonfiction books may appeal more to those who like intricate tales.

Visit the library to try out different types of reading material. It's free! Also explore the Internet for various reading sources.

Finding the type of reading material that is right for your personality and interests will make reading fun, will lead to better reading skills, and will even make the reading you are forced to do more productive.

▌▐▌▌ INTERACTIVE EXERCISE

Use the dictionary to find a word you don't know that uses the word part listed below. Write the meaning of the word part, the word, and the definition. If your dictionary has the etymology (history) of the word, see how the word part relates to the meaning, and write the etymology after the definition.

Word Part	Meaning	Word	Definition and Etymology
EXAMPLE:			
ir-	*not*	*irrefragable*	*incapable of being refuted or disproved*
			Latin in-, not + refragari, to oppose
1. *clar-*			
2. *gen-*			

Word Part	Meaning	Word	Definition and Etymology

3. *il-* _____

_____

_____

_____

4. *in-* _____

_____

_____

_____

5. *mal-* _____

_____

_____

_____

▋▍▋▋ WHERE DID IT COME FROM?

Villainous (Chapter 12): comes from villain, which in Latin was *villanus* "a farm servant." *Villanus* came from *villa* "a farm." In the Middle Ages a villain was simply a peasant or person who worked on a farm owned by the lord of the area. Because peasants were not cultured or educated, the meaning of villain shifted downward and eventually became "an evil person," and villainous came to mean "evil or wicked."

Dismal (Chapter 16): comes from the Latin *dies mali. Dies* is the plural of "day" and *mali* the plural of "evil." The word meant "unlucky days." There were two days in each month that were thought to be unfavorable, and it was considered best not to start anything important on those days. For example, in January the two days were the 1st and 25th. The days were even marked on calendars during the Middles Ages. It is easy to see how unlucky days could develop into today's meaning of dismal: "miserable, depressing."

© 2007 Pearson Education, Inc.

14 Fitness

A Healthy Body

A Healthy Body

A healthy body isn't impossible to achieve. First you have to **confront** what is keeping you from being as healthy as you should be. Are you eating too much or exercising too little? Or both? 5

Getting in shape isn't a **fluke**; it takes hard work and **dedication**. But your workouts do not have to be **grueling** either. Find an activity you like to do and 10 set up a workout **regimen**. Put your workouts on your calendar: walk Monday, Wednesday, and Friday from 9 a.m. to 10 a.m. Don't let a setback **fluster** you. If you forget to walk on Wednesday, don't 15 give up. Walk on Friday and you will be fine.

Some people like activities that involve **opposition**. If you need to compete with someone, pick a sport like tennis. Having 20 people to play against can keep you training. Make your activity as **intense** as you can handle. People handle stress differently. Some people like to compete with others and some don't. Do what 25 makes you happy, so you will keep doing it.

Also watch what you eat as part of your health regimen. Eat a balanced diet and eat in **moderation**. By controlling what you eat and maintaining a steady exercise program, 30 you will **triumph** and have the body you desire.

Are you eating too much or exercising too little? Or both?

▌▐▐▌ PREDICTING

For each set, write the definition on the line next to the word to which it belongs. If you are unsure, return to the reading on page 86, and underline any context clues you find. After you've made your predictions, check your answers against the Word List on page 91. Place a checkmark in the box next to each word whose definition you missed. These are the words you'll want to study closely.

SET ONE

exhausting	a lucky chance	to face head on	a plan
the state of being devoted to a cause			

❑ 1. **confront** (line 3) _____

❑ 2. **fluke** (line 7) _____

❑ 3. **dedication** (line 8) _____

❑ 4. **grueling** (line 9) _____

❑ 5. **regimen** (line 11) _____

SET TWO

a state of confusion	avoidance of extremes	to an extreme degree
to win	contestant one is matched against	

❑ 6. **fluster** (line 14) _____

❑ 7. **opposition** (line 18) _____

❑ 8. **intense** (line 21) _____

❑ 9. **moderation** (line 28) _____

❑ 10. **triumph** (line 30) _____

▌▐▐▌ SELF-TESTS

1 Put a T for true or F for false next to each sentence.

_____ 1. When confronted with a problem, it can be a good idea to think about it for awhile before making a decision.

_____ 2. Dedications in books are often addressed to parents or other family members.

_____ 3. Winning the lottery is a fluke.

_____ 4. Spending a relaxing day at home would fluster most people.

_____ 5. Climbing one of the highest mountains in the world would be grueling.

_____ 6. Writing a thousand-page book is an intense experience.

_____ 7. A parent and teenager agreeing on the time to come home from a date shows opposition.

_____ 8. Eating anything you want shows a strict dietary regimen.

_____ 9. Buying ten new outfits every day shows moderation in spending habits.

_____ 10. Finding a cure for cancer would be a triumph.

© 2007 Pearson Education, Inc.

2 Finish these headlines using the vocabulary words. Use each word once.

VOCABULARY LIST

confronts	dedicates	fluke	flustered	grueling
intense	opposition	regimen	moderation	triumphs

1. Huge Sports _____ : Worst Team in the League Beats Last Year's Champs!

2. Top Golfer-_____ by Photographers-Yells at Crowd

3. Tour de France Update: Ten Riders Fade in _____ Mountain Stage

4. The _____ that Wins — Jordan's Training Secrets for Guaranteed Success

5. _____ Is the Key to Avoiding Burnout When Training for a Marathon

6. Wimbledon Veteran Faces Tough _____ from Newcomer

7. *New Information on Steroid Use _____ the NFL*

8. Pitcher _____ His Talents to Youth Camp

9. *Gymnast _____ : From Spinal Injury to Gold Medal*

10. _____ Wind Delays Slalom Events

3 In each group, circle the word that does not have a connection to the other three words.

1. upset	fluster	calm	confuse
2. discipline	uncontrolled	plan	regimen
3. intense	strong	extreme	weak
4. lucky	fluke	misfortune	accident
5. refreshing	tiring	grueling	exhausting
6. opposition	cooperation	competition	disagreement
7. commit	dedicate	devote	avoid
8. mild	limit	extreme	moderation
9. retreat	face	confront	brave
10. triumph	lose	win	overcome

4 For each set, replace the underlined synonym or definition with the correct vocabulary word. Use each word once.

SET ONE

VOCABULARY LIST

flustered	dedication	fluke	triumph	regimen

1. "I write down what I eat every day, and I go to the gym four days a week. I really feel healthier now that I am following this <u>plan</u>." _____

2. "We were down by two points and won just as the clock ran out. We deserved to <u>win</u> since we were able to overcome injuries and bad calls by the referees." _____

3. "Welcome to the <u>opening</u> of Lewiston Hall, which honors one of the first graduates of this university." _____

4. "What a <u>lucky chance</u>. You didn't study for the test and Professor Winston was absent. I heard that he hasn't missed a day in the last seven years." _____

5. "This dance step has me <u>confused</u>. Every time I try it I fall down." _____

SET TWO

VOCABULARY LIST

moderation	grueling	intense	opposition	confront

6. "The <u>other contestants</u> should be here soon, but I understand they won't be hard to beat." _____

7. "Don't force the stretch; <u>control</u> is the key to yoga. Try to avoid extremes." _____

8. "I need <u>to face</u> my problem: I am a chocoholic." _____

9. "This run is <u>exhausting</u>. It seems like we have been climbing hills all day." _____

10. "I don't like to play against him. His desire to win is <u>too extreme</u>; I just want to have fun." _____

© 2007 Pearson Education, Inc.

Answer the following questions as they apply to your life:

1. What have you shown dedication toward? _____

2. What most flusters you? _____

3. What was the most grueling experience you've had? _____

   _____

4. What is the toughest opposition you've faced? _____

5. What is something you need to do in moderation? _____

6. What is the toughest problem you have confronted? _____

7. What has been the biggest fluke in your life? _____

8. What is the most intense experience you've had? _____

   _____

9. What is the hardest regimen you've had to follow? _____

   _____

10. What is your greatest triumph? _____

   _____

HINT

Two Essentials

They may seem like obvious points, but it doesn't hurt to be reminded that getting a good night's rest and drinking plenty of water will help your brain and body perform at their best.

1. Sleep: Staying up late to study now and then won't hurt you, but making late nights a continual practice may do damage to your education. Most adults need 7–8 hours of sleep each night to function well during the day. You should wake up ready to face the day's challenges. Power naps can also help. Sleeping for thirty minutes in the afternoon can make the rest of your day more productive. Studies have found that people get the most benefit from naps taken between 2:00–3:00 p.m.
2. Water: Drinking 6–8 eight-ounce glasses of water a day will help your system work efficiently. Water keeps you energized and helps your muscles work better. Drink before your body tells you it is thirsty, so you don't get dehydrated.

▮▮▮ WORD LIST

confront
[kən frunt′]
v. to face head on

dedication
[ded′ ə kā′ shən]
n. 1. the state of being devoted to a cause
2. a message attached to a book or other artistic work to show thanks or respect
3. a ceremony to open a building

dedicate
[ded′ ə kāt′]
v. to devote

fluke
[flo͞ok]
n. a lucky chance; accidental good luck

fluster
[flus′ tûr]
n. a state of confusion
v. to upset; to cause confused behavior

grueling
[gro͞o′ ə ling]
adj. tiring; exhausting

intense
[in tens′]
adj. to an extreme degree; deep

moderation
[mod′ ər ā′ shən]
n. avoidance of extremes; control

opposition
[äp′ ə zish′ ən]
n. 1. a contestant one is matched against
2. conflict; disagreement

regimen
[rej′ ə mən, -men′]
n. a plan; discipline

triumph
[trī′ əmpf]
v. to win; to overcome
n. the joy of victory

▮▮▮ WORDS TO WATCH

Which words would you like to practice with a bit more? Pick 3–5 words to study and list them below. Write the word, its definition, and compose your own sentence using the word correctly. This extra practice could be the final touch to learning a word.

Word	Definition	Your Sentence
1. _____	_____	_____
_____		
2. _____	_____	_____
_____		
3. _____	_____	_____
_____		
4. _____	_____	_____
_____		
5. _____	_____	_____
_____		

© 2007 Pearson Education, Inc.

15 Personal Finance

A Healthy Wallet

They're out there! About 80% of the households in the United States have at least one credit card and several Americans say they have close to eight cards. That is a lot of credit available, and it
5 has led to a **precarious** situation for many Americans. Too many people have **overextended** themselves. The average credit card **debt** for Americans in 2004 was near $2,000, and some people have over $10,000 in debt. Don't be a vic-
10 tim of credit card debt.

Staying Out of Debt

It all begins with **attitude**. You have to believe that living debt free is a beneficial way to manage your life. You have to want to keep more of your money instead of paying it to credit card companies. First, figure out how much money you bring home each month after taxes. Then add up your expenses, such as rent or mortgage, car payments, gas, insurance, utility bills, food, and clothing. How much money is left is what
15 you have to spend. Next consider the benefits of **investing** some of your money in savings accounts, retirement accounts, or the stock market. Then use the rest for fun. If you don't create a budget, you could end up spending a lot more for an item than you might expect. For example, if you buy a $2,000 big screen television with your credit card and you pay the minimum each month (about 2% of the outstanding balance or in this case $40 to start) and your interest rate is 14% (the average credit card interest rate for 2002
20 was almost 19%), it would take you 242 months (20 years 2 months) to pay off your debt (and that's if you bought nothing else with that card). You would have paid an additional $2,354.76 to the credit card company for that television. Here is where attitude pays off. Think about whether you really need a big screen television or if you need it right now or whether you can make more than the minimum payment each month. Since the future can be **uncertain** (layoffs and injuries are two potential problems), it is reassuring
25 not having to worry about finding the money to put toward credit card debt every month.

Getting Out of Debt

If you already have money you owe on your cards, the first recommendation most credit counselors will **prescribe** is stop using your cards. You need to get a handle on your spending, and you can't do so if you keep adding to your debt. Next, talk to a **reputable** credit counselor if you have serious debt. Find someone you can trust. Look at all your **options** before you decide what to do. You will have some choices to
30 make. You will likely need to dispose of a few of your cards. If you have eight cards or more get rid of some of them. You only realistically need two. Next you may want to transfer any balances on high interest rate cards (over 20%) to lower interest rate cards (less than 14%). Most importantly, you need to look at your budget and carefully think about the things you really need.

Everyone can **acquire** better spending habits. Credit cards have their benefits: they are convenient to
35 use, they give you a borrowing history useful for bigger purchases (a car or a house) later on, and you can even get rewards like airline miles, merchandise, or cash. Don't give up on credit cards, but learn to use them wisely. Then you will have money to invest in savings and build toward a healthy financial future.

▊▊▊ PREDICTING

For each set, write the definition on the line next to the word to which it belongs. If you are unsure, return to the reading on page 92, and underline any context clues you find. After you've made your predictions, check your answers against the Word List on page 97. Place a checkmark in the box next to each word whose definition you missed. These are the words you'll want to study closely.

return to the reading on page 92 ... check your answers against the Word List on page 97.

SET ONE

| using something for profit | insecure | a way of thinking or behaving |
| something owed | promised more than can be delivered | |

- ☐ 1. **precarious** (line 5) _____
- ☐ 2. **overextended** (line 6) _____
- ☐ 3. **debt** (line 7) _____
- ☐ 4. **attitude** (line 11) _____
- ☐ 5. **investing** (line 15) _____

SET TWO

| trustworthy | to obtain | choices | not known |
| to give as a rule or guide | | | |

- ☐ 6. **uncertain** (line 24) _____
- ☐ 7. **prescribe** (line 27) _____
- ☐ 8. **reputable** (line 28) _____
- ☐ 9. **options** (line 29) _____
- ☐ 10. **acquire** (line 34) _____

▊▊▊ SELF-TESTS

1 In each group, circle the word that does not have a connection to the other three words.

1. advise	recommend	oppose	prescribe
2. option	limitation	choice	alternative
3. respectable	trustworthy	reputable	dishonorable
4. sure	uncertain	hesitant	undecided
5. insecure	precarious	stable	shaky
6. remove	supply	empower	invest

© 2007 Pearson Education, Inc.

7. get	acquire	give	obtain
8. exceed	limit	overextend	strain
9. outlook	attitude	thoughts	unconscious
10. possession	obligation	owe	debt

2 Finish the analogies. See Completing Analogies on page 5 for instructions and practice. Use each word once.

VOCABULARY LIST

prescribes	debt	acquire	attitude	overextend
precarious	uncertain	option	invest	reputable

1. hungry : full :: sure : _____
2. eat : a meal :: _____ : knowledge
3. deadline : work late :: _____ : frustration
4. math : subject :: the blue or the red : _____
5. red : rose :: positive : _____
6. chef : cooks :: doctor : _____
7. tall : big :: obligation : _____
8. devote : energy :: _____ : time
9. simple : elaborate :: dishonest : _____
10. stealing a purse : villainous :: standing on the edge of a cliff : _____

3 For Set One match each term with its synonym. For Set Two match each term with its antonym.

SYNONYMS

SET ONE

_____ 1. attitude   a. honorable
_____ 2. option   b. doubtful
_____ 3. reputable   c. view
_____ 4. prescribe   d. choice
_____ 5. uncertain   e. suggest

ANTONYMS

SET TWO

_____ 6. overextend   f. safe
_____ 7. acquire   g. conserve
_____ 8. debt   h. misuse
_____ 9. precarious   i. give
_____ 10. invest   j. savings

4 Finish the reading using the vocabulary words. Use each word once.

VOCABULARY LIST

acquiring	reputable	overextend	uncertain	debt
options	prescribed	investing	precarious	attitude

My financial situation is (1)_____ right now because I'm almost broke. I spent more over the last six months than I made. I was (2)_____ about what I should do until last week. On Saturday I attended a financial planning seminar. The instructors seemed quite (3)_____; I felt I could trust them as they both had over ten years experience in financial planning. They suggested I write down every penny I spend, and then evaluate my spending habits. I started by listing my monthly expenses for rent, car payment, and utility bills. Then I looked at other things I have recently bought like a $1,000 ring for my girlfriend for Valentine's Day. I did not need to get her such an expensive gift.

My (4)_____ concerning money has changed. I used to enjoy it and now I fear going into (5)_____. I actually used to think about (6)_____ in stocks; now I worry about how I'm ever going to get caught up with my payments. I have been worried about (7)_____ more money, rather than considering how I actually spend the money I already make. The instructors pointed out that there are several (8)_____ when deciding what to do with one's money, but first a person needs to have money to invest. They (9)_____ practical solutions on how to use the money I already have to plan for my future. I am no longer going to (10)_____ myself financially. I see where I have gone too far in the past, and I am ready to work toward a healthy financial life.

© 2007 Pearson Education, Inc.

Write two responses for each of the following topics.

1. What are you uncertain about?

    1. _____ 2. _____

2. What are you most interested in acquiring in life?

    1. _____ 2. _____

3. What are some attitudes people have towards money?

    1. _____ 2. _____

4. What activities would you prescribe for someone who is depressed?

    1. _____ 2. _____

5. How do people overextend themselves?

    1. _____ 2. _____

6. What do people invest in?

    1. _____ 2. _____

7. What would a precarious situation be?

    1. _____ 2. _____

8. What options have you been faced with recently?

    1. _____ 2. _____

9. What can people do to stay out of debt?

    1. _____ 2. _____

10. What qualities would a reputable person have?

    1. _____ 2. _____

HINT

Shades of Meaning

Learning new vocabulary is more than learning synonyms. While some words you learn may be similar to other words you know and may be used in place of another word, every word is unique. Good writers choose their words carefully. Words have different shades of meaning, and conscientious writers think about those differences when picking a word to use. A careful reader also responds to those differences in meaning. In some cases the differences are slight, such as "On Sundays I eat a big dinner" or "On Sundays I eat a large dinner." But replacing "big" or "large" with "huge" or "gigantic" (both synonyms for "big") does alter the image of how much food the person is eating. Some synonyms have even bigger differences. For the sentence, "The clever woman found a way to get out of debt," "clever" could be replaced with the synonyms "smart" or "crafty." The reader would have a different reaction to the woman depending on whether the writer selected "smart" or "crafty." When reading or writing, pay attention to the diverse ways words can be used.

◼◼◼◼ WORD LIST

acquire
[ə kwīr′]
v. to get possession of; to obtain

attitude
[at′ ə tōōd′]
n. a way of thinking or behaving; outlook

debt
[det]
n. something owed; an obligation

invest
[in vest′]
v. to use something for profit (for example, money, time)

option
[op′ shən]
n. choosing; choice; alternative; the thing chosen

overextend
[ō′ vûr ik stend′]
v. to promise more (money, time, etc.) than one can deliver; to try to do too much

precarious
[pri kâr′ ē əs]
adj. 1. insecure; dangerously lacking security
2. subject to change

prescribe
[pri skrīb′]
v. to give as a rule or guide; to recommend the use of

reputable
[rep′ yə tə bəl]
adj. respectable; honorable; trustworthy

uncertain
[un′ sûrt′ n]
adj. not known; doubtful; undecided

◼◼◼◼ WORDS TO WATCH

Which words would you like to practice with a bit more? Pick 3–5 words to study and list them below. Write the word, its definition, and compose your own sentence using the word correctly. This extra practice could be the final touch to learning a word.

Word	Definition	Your Sentence
1. _____	_____	_____
_____	_____	_____
2. _____	_____	_____
_____	_____	_____
3. _____	_____	_____
_____	_____	_____
4. _____	_____	_____
_____	_____	_____
5. _____	_____	_____
_____	_____	_____

© 2007 Pearson Education, Inc.

16 The World

A Healthy Environment

June 25
It is the second night of my environmental awareness retreat. We have been camped out in the forest to learn how the world is changing. I didn't know what to **anticipate** when I signed up. I hoped it wasn't going to be a **dismal** weekend
5   of complaining about how badly humans are treating the planet. And it hasn't been. There is hope for the Earth! The instructors have been great in showing us what we can do from following **trends** such as recycling to writing key officials in Washington to **stimulate** their interest in environmental legislation. If we want to save the planet, we must not be **impassive**. Some of the damage isn't **irrevocable**.
10   Today we paddled on the river and were shown how cleanup efforts rescued the river from the damages of pollution and illegal dumping. With the right efforts we can clean up contaminated streams and save endangered animals. I can't wait for tomorrow's activities.

June 26
15   Today the instructors focused on how environmental issues are **global** concerns. For example, the **depletion** of the ozone layer is a worldwide problem, and the loss of protection that layer provides may lead to health difficulties
20   everywhere. I am an **avid** fan of nature, and I want to help keep the planet beautiful. It has been so peaceful here in the forest; I don't want places like this to disappear. What I learned most is that if we all **cooperate**, we can have a
25   healthy environment! All we need to do is work together.

▌▌▐▐▌ PREDICTING

For each set, write the definition on the line next to the word to which it belongs. If you are unsure, return to the reading on page 98 and underline any context clues you find. After you've made your predictions, check your answers against the Word List on page 103. Place a checkmark in the box next to each word whose definition you missed. These are the words you'll want to study closely.

SET ONE

miserable	to excite	to look forward to	having a lack of interest
a leaning			

- ❏ 1. **anticipate** (line 4) _____
- ❏ 2. **dismal** (line 4) _____
- ❏ 3. **trend** (line 7) _____
- ❏ 4. **stimulate** (line 8) _____
- ❏ 5. **impassive** (line 9) _____

SET TWO

enthusiastic	unchangeable	to work together	reduction
international			

- ❏ 6. **irrevocable** (line 9) _____
- ❏ 7. **global** (line 16) _____
- ❏ 8. **depletion** (line 17) _____
- ❏ 9. **avid** (line 20) _____
- ❏ 10. **cooperate** (line 24) _____

▌▌▐▐▌ SELF-TESTS

1 Finish the sentences using the vocabulary words below. Use each word once.

VOCABULARY LIST

anticipating	avid	trends	impassive	stimulate
global	cooperation	dismal	irrevocable	depletion

1. I don't like to follow the latest fashion _____, but my sister does. She reads several fashion magazines.
2. My dad is a(n) _____ reader of mysteries; he has over two thousand mystery books.
3. My brother's day was _____ after he got two flat tires on his bike.

© 2007 Pearson Education, Inc.

VOCABULARY LIST

anticipating	avid	trends	impassive	stimulate
global	cooperation	dismal	irrevocable	depletion

4. Taking a trip around the world would be a _____ experience.

5. There has been a rapid _____ of snacks in the kitchen since Anthony got home from college.

6. Cheering someone on in a race can _____ the person to do better.

7. My nephew is eagerly _____ his birthday; he can't wait to see if he will get the race car set he asked for.

8. My neighbor is _____; he never joins in any of the activities we have on the block.

9. Cleaning the house together shows _____.

10. My instructor said my grade was _____; there was nothing I could do to change it.

2 Put a T for true or F for false next to each statement.

_____ 1. A lot of people are avid about sports.

_____ 2. A politician tries to stimulate interest in his or her campaign.

_____ 3. Cell phones are a fast-growing trend.

_____ 4. Most people consider a sunny day dismal.

_____ 5. People can make comments during a fight that can cause irrevocable damage to a relationship.

_____ 6. There has been a depletion of the Earth's overall population in the last two hundred years.

_____ 7. At the airport most people anticipate some sort of delay.

_____ 8. If a child refuses to help pick up his toys, he shows he knows how to cooperate.

_____ 9. Walking to my neighborhood park is an example of a global activity.

_____10. Shouting for one's favorite team to win and crying when they lose would be the actions of an impassive person.

3 Circle the word that best completes the sentence.

1. I am disappointed in the (global, dismal) turnout for the meeting; I guess the bad weather scared people away.

2. To (stimulate, cooperate) interest in the upcoming concert, the band marched around campus during the lunch hour for a week.

3. I am an (irrevocable, avid) bicyclist; I ride at least thirty miles every day.

4. The (global, avid) meeting on how to achieve worldwide peace will be held in Berlin this May with over one hundred countries represented.

5. There has been a (depletion, trend) in our water supply because we had so little rain this year.

6. We (cooperate, anticipate) a full house at the meeting; the water conservation issue has upset a lot of people.

7. The committee assignments are (impassive, irrevocable). We can't have people constantly moving from one place to another; you must stay on your committee until the job is done.

8. I wonder what the latest fashion (trend, depletion) will be; I hope it isn't silly like platform shoes.

9. Because everyone was able to (anticipate, cooperate), the project was completed a month ahead of schedule.

10. The public has become so (impassive, avid) that almost no one votes anymore.

4 Finish the story by using the vocabulary words. Use each word once.

VOCABULARY LIST

dismal	avid	irrevocable	depletion	impassive
trends	cooperate	stimulate	globally	anticipated

Keri wanted to stop being (1)_____ and start helping the environment. She decided to begin with her neighborhood. She didn't want people to see the situation as being (2)_____. She wanted to show that environmental problems are not (3)_____; she wanted to show her neighbors that people can change the world. Keri decided that to (4)_____ an interest in environmental issues she would have an Environmental Fair with food, games, and information booths at the neighborhood park. She knew there were some (5)_____ environmentalists in her neighborhood like Dan. Dan recycled everything, drove an electric car, and joined protests to save endangered animals. Keri went to Dan's house to discuss the Fair.

"Keri, have you (6)_____ all the problems you will have putting on this event?"

"I know it won't be easy, but since it will benefit the Earth, I am willing to work hard. I also know there are people who will (7)_____ with me in organizing this event—like you."

"Okay, Keri, you have my participation. Let's think (8)_____ and then narrow down our ideas to the neighborhood. We can have a display on the (9)_____ of resources worldwide and then show our neighbors how they can help to save those resources."

"One of the (10)_____ that I want to support is recycling, with bins for paper, plastic, and cans all over the park. Maybe the bins can even stay after the Fair."

"That's a great idea. I have some thoughts on the food we can offer and fun environmental games. Let's sit down and start planning. I am proud of you, Keri, for taking this on!"

© 2007 Pearson Education, Inc.

Below is a section from an imaginary textbook about the environment. Complete the exercises to gain practice in using the vocabulary words.

THE ENVIRONMENT AND YOU: LESSON I

What do you know about the environment? Test your environmental awareness by answering the following questions. These matters will be discussed in the rest of the text.

Exercise I. List two global environmental problems. Example:

depletion of forests worldwide

1. _____

2. _____

Exercise II. What do you consider the most dismal situation involving the environment? Do you think it is irrevocable?

_____

_____

Exercise III. List two ways you can stimulate people to become avid environmentalists. Think about current trends, such as recycling, to develop your list.

1. _____   2. _____

Exercise IV. People are often impassive and it can be hard to get them to cooperate. List two problems you would anticipate in getting people involved.

1. _____   2. _____

HINT

A Comfortable Spot

To concentrate on what you are reading, you need to find the right environment. For most people that means turning off the television and radio. Most people concentrate better in a quiet space. You can experiment to see if you are the kind of person who actually concentrates better with some background noise. Also look for a place with good light; you don't want to strain your eyes. You should be comfortable, so find a chair you like, or if you need to take notes, you may want to sit at a table. For some people, especially if they are reading for fun, sitting outside in a park or the backyard provides a pleasant place to read. See what works best for you depending on what material you are reading. Change your environment if you find you can't focus on what you are reading.

▌▌▌▌ WORD LIST

anticipate
[an tis′ ə pāt′]

v. to look forward to; to expect

avid
[av′ id]

adj. eager; enthusiastic

cooperate
[kō äp′ ər āt]

v. to work together; to agree

depletion
[di plē′ shən]

n. the act of decreasing something; reduction

dismal
[diz′ məl]

adj. miserable; depressing; dull

global
[glō′ bəl]

adj. involving the entire Earth; international

impassive
[im pas′ iv]

adj. having a lack of interest; not showing emotion; expressionless

irrevocable
[i rev′ ə kə bəl]

adj. unchangeable; final; permanent

stimulate
[stim′ yə lāt′]

v. to excite; to inspire; to cause . to do

trend
[trend]

n. a general direction in which something tends to move; a leaning

▌▌▌▌ WORDS TO WATCH

Which words would you like to practice with a bit more? Pick 3–5 words to study and list them below. Write the word, its definition, and compose your own sentence using the word correctly. This extra practice could be the final touch to learning a word.

Word	Definition	Your Sentence
1. _____	_____	_____
_____	_____	_____
2. _____	_____	_____
_____	_____	_____
3. _____	_____	_____
_____	_____	_____
4. _____	_____	_____
_____	_____	_____
5. _____	_____	_____
_____	_____	_____

© 2007 Pearson Education, Inc.

Focus on Chapters 10–16

The following activities give you a chance to interact some more with the vocabulary words you've been learning. By looking at art, taking tests, answering questions, doing a crossword puzzle, and acting, you will see which words you know well and which you still need to work with.

1. _____

2. _____

3. _____

4. _____

5. _____

6. _____

7. _____

8. _____

9. _____

10. _____

11. _____

12._____

 ART

Match each picture on page 104 to one of the following vocabulary words. Use each word once.

VOCABULARY LIST

depletion	options	novice	appreciation
opposition	precarious	manuscript	monotonous
superlative	burden	triumph	villainous

 SELF-TESTS

1 Pick the word that best completes each sentence.

1. I didn't _____ my homework taking so long. Now I don't know if I will finish.

    a. acquire   b. anticipate   c. generate   d. cooperate

2. I hate it when a movie gets a lot of _____. A movie usually can't live up to my expectations when so much has been said about it.

    a. debt   b. attitude   c. contention   d. hype

3. I enjoy _____ that has the main character battling with nature.

    a. triumph   b. critic   c. fiction   d. novice

4. My brother is a _____; he is always dreaming up impractical inventions.

    a. visionary   b. novice   c. burden   d. fluke

5. I am angry at Julian for putting me in such a _____. He was supposed to meet my train and he isn't here, and now I don't know what to do.

    a. category   b. predicament   c. buff   d. depletion

6. I was so proud when the committee decided to _____ the award on me; I had worked hard on the project, and I was pleased to have my efforts recognized.

    a. invest   b. elaborate   c. stimulate   d. bestow

7. My _____ have grown so big, I'm not sure I can ever pay them off.

    a. blunders   b. chronicles   c. debts   d. dedications

8. Lisa found skydiving to be an _____ experience; it was extremely exciting.

    a. uncertain   b. intense   c. avid   d. elaborate

9. I considered all my _____ before I bought my car; I am happy with my choice.

    a. contentions   b. chronicles   c. trends   d. options

10. I don't _____ easily, but when I couldn't find my research paper, I got upset.

    a. fluster   b. overextend   c. cooperate   d. jeopardize

© 2007 Pearson Education, Inc.

2 Finish the reading using the vocabulary words below. Use each word once.

VOCABULARY LIST

associated	categories	dedication	contention	elaborate
generate	invest	qualify	sufficient	precarious

BIG PLANS

The meeting on what to do for the

(1)_____ of the college's new Inspiration

Garden really got crazy. The garden was built as a

place where students could sit and think in peaceful

surroundings. The plans for the opening started to

get (2)_____. People wanted to bring in

dancers and rock bands and offer food from local

restaurants. There was even the suggestion of a

dance contest and the finalists would

(3)_____ for a drawing for a reserved parking space for the semester. Someone finally said

that we didn't have (4)_____ funds to put on such a complicated event. Someone suggested

we could (5)_____ the money through donations. Someone else mentioned that no one had

the time to (6)_____ in getting the money. Then there was the (7)_____ that such

a gathering didn't fit in with the quiet atmosphere of the garden. The possibility of our agreeing on

what to do seemed quite (8)_____. Finally, we decided to put the ideas we thought were

important into a few (9)_____ and focus on those items. By the end of the meeting we had

planned a simple, but meaningful, event. I was proud to be (10)_____ with the planning

committee.

Answer the following questions to further test your understanding of the vocabulary words.

1. What are two trends that you think have been silly?

   _____   _____

2. What are two ways you could jeopardize your doing well in a class?

   _____   _____

3. List one of the preliminary steps for preparing to go to college. _____

   _____

4. What sport are you avid about? Or whom do you know who is an avid sports fan?

   _____

5. What activity do you consider grueling? _____

6. What are two items you would especially want to buy from a reputable dealer?

   _____   _____

7. What event would you like to read the chronicles of? _____

8. What kind of buff are you? _____

   _____

9. List an event or activity that you would consider a fluke. _____

10. What would you prescribe someone do to relieve stress? _____

   _____

© 2007 Pearson Education, Inc.

CROSSWORD PUZZLE

Use the following words to complete the crossword puzzle. Use each word once.

VOCABULARY LIST

associated	attitude	clarity	dismal	global
irrevocable	maladjusted	manuscript	moderation	nettle
novice	overextend	regimen	stimulate	superfluous

Across

2. avoidance of extremes
4. a written document
6. outlook
7. clearness
9. related to
12. to annoy
13. a plan
14. international
15. emotionally unstable

Down

1. a beginner
3. to try to do too much
5. to excite
8. final
10. more than is needed
11. depressing

HINT

Use Them

Take an important step to make the words you study part of your vocabulary: Use them outside the classroom. When you feel that you understand a word, use it as often as you can in speaking and writing. If you continue to use it—even if you don't feel comfortable doing so at first—the word will become part of your active vocabulary. *It will belong to you.* Learning vocabulary is about using words, not memorizing definitions. Try the words out on friends and family; they will be impressed with what you have learned and so will you.

COLLABORATIVE ACTIVITY: DRAMA

Charades: You may be given one of the following words to act out in class or you may want to do this activity with a study group. Think about how these words could be demonstrated without speaking. The other people will try to guess what word you are showing.

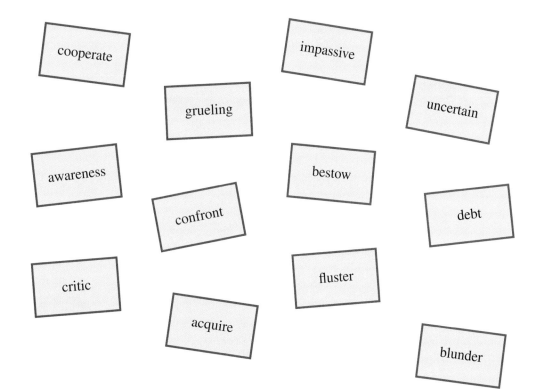

© 2007 Pearson Education, Inc.

CHAPTER 18 Personalities

As the Cookie Crumbles

How do we know who we are? What the future holds? The answer is simple: we have only to open a fortune cookie to find our true personalities. Do any of these fortunes sound like they could be yours?

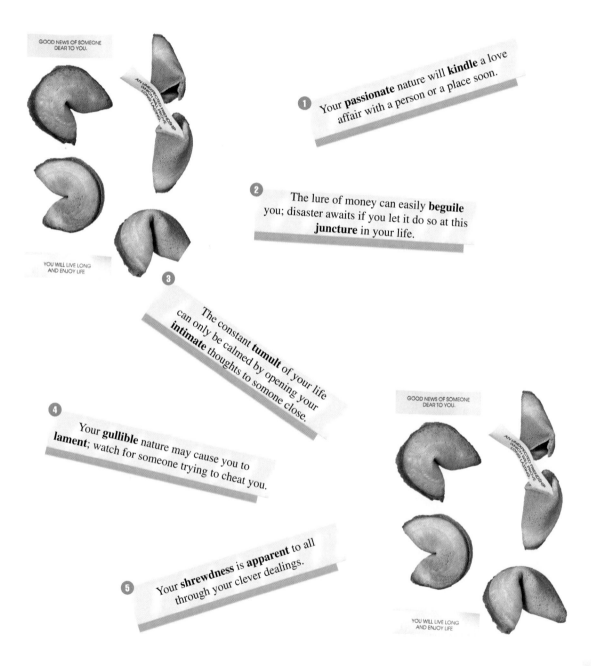

GOOD NEWS OF SOMEONE DEAR TO YOU.

AN UNEXPECTED FRIENDSHIP WILL SOON BE STARTING

YOU WILL LIVE LONG AND ENJOY LIFE

1. Your **passionate** nature will **kindle** a love affair with a person or a place soon.

2. The lure of money can easily **beguile** you; disaster awaits if you let it do so at this **juncture** in your life.

3. The constant **tumult** of your life can only be calmed by opening your **intimate** thoughts to somone close.

4. Your **gullible** nature may cause you to **lament**; watch for someone trying to cheat you.

5. Your **shrewdness** is **apparent** to all through your clever dealings.

GOOD NEWS OF SOMEONE DEAR TO YOU.

AN UNEXPECTED FRIENDSHIP WILL SOON BE STARTING

YOU WILL LIVE LONG AND ENJOY LIFE

▌▌▌▌ PREDICTING

For each set, write the definition on the line next to the word to which it belongs. If you are unsure, return to the reading on page 110, and underline any context clues you find. After you've made your predictions, check your answers against the Word List on page 115. Place a checkmark in the box next to each word whose definition you missed. These are the words you'll want to study closely.

SET ONE

a stage	having strong emotions	to entice	disorder	to inspire

❑ 1. **passionate** (fortune 1) _____

❑ 2. **kindle** (fortune 1) _____

❑ 3. **beguile** (fortune 2) _____

❑ 4. **juncture** (fortune 2) _____

❑ 5. **tumult** (fortune 3) _____

SET TWO

to express grief	of a close or private nature	clear	intelligence	easily fooled

❑ 6. **intimate** (fortune 3) _____

❑ 7. **gullible** (fortune 4) _____

❑ 8. **lament** (fortune 4) _____

❑ 9. **shrewdness** (fortune 5) _____

❑ 10. **apparent** (fortune 5) _____

▌▌▌▌ SELF-TESTS

1 Match the vocabulary word to the situation it best fits. Use the underlined context clues to help you make the connections. Context clues may be synonyms, antonyms, examples, or the general meaning of a sentence.

SET ONE

_____ 1. The man's singing charmed Lauretta; she started to attend all his concerts.

_____ 2. Brian's brother knocked on the door and ran away six times; his brother got up to answer it every time.

_____ 3. Because Shauna is her close friend, Stephanie shared a family secret with her.

_____ 4. Bob is grieving over his hamster's death.

_____ 5. The crowd rushed the ticket window when it was announced that only ten tickets were left for the big game.

a. gullible

b. lament

c. tumult

d. intimate

e. beguile

© 2007 Pearson Education, Inc.

_____ 6. The man turned a $50 investment into $5,000.

        f. kindle

_____ 7. At this point in his life, Reginald thought he was too young to get married.

        g. juncture

_____ 8. The math major was enthusiastic about her homework. She stayed up all night solving equations, and she wanted more.

        h. apparent

        i. passionate

_____ 9. After vacationing for three weeks together, the closeness awakened deeper feelings between Amelia and Karl.

        j. shrewdness

_____ 10. Mom and Dad came home and saw the pile of paper plates in the trash and the soda stains on the rug; it was clear there had been a party.

2 Complete the sentences using the word list below. Use each word once.

VOCABULARY LIST

beguile	kindled	intimate	tumult	lamented
gullible	juncture	passionate	shrewdness	apparent

1. At this _____ we need to take a break. Everyone is so tired we haven't had a good idea in over an hour.

2. It is _____ that you like to eat Chinese food; you have gone to four Chinese restaurants this week.

3. A _____ student will be eager to study.

4. She shared the most _____ details of her love life with her best friend.

5. The student showed his _____ when he took the time to study instead of going to the party.

6. Don't let a salesman _____ you; research a product before you shop for it.

7. After he failed the test, the student _____ going to the party instead of studying.

8. The _____ in my life will be over when this crazy semester ends.

9. Because of the student's _____ nature, he believed the teacher when she said, "I like it when students come to class unprepared." The next day he felt foolish when he didn't bring his textbook.

10. The campers _____ a fire to keep themselves warm when the sun set.

3 In each group, circle the word that does not have a connection to the other three words.

1. stage   moment   eternity   juncture

2. grieve   laugh   lament   cry

3. confused   clear   apparent   plain

4. excited   passionate   calm   loving

5. believing	trustful	gullible	suspicious
6. peace	confusion	tumult	uproar
7. intimate	private	close	public
8. wisdom	intelligence	stupidity	shrewdness
9. inspire	kindle	excite	extinguish
10. beguile	lure	repel	charm

4 For each set, answer the questions about the quotations. Look for context clues to help you. Use each word once.

VOCABULARY LIST

apparent	shrewdness	beguile	intimate	passionate

SET ONE

1. "My sister, Daphne, was able to turn a run-down restaurant into a gourmet café. I admire her financial skills." What kind of intelligence does Daphne have? _____

2. "I write my private thoughts in a diary." What kind of thoughts does the person write? _____

3. "Roberto is enthusiastic about cooking spicy food; he loves to make hot dishes." How does Roberto feel about cooking? _____

4. "Anyone could easily see that their marriage wasn't going to last; they had nothing in common." How obvious was it to people that the marriage was going to fail? _____

5. "The pastries in the window enticed me into getting some." What did the pastries do to the person? _____

VOCABULARY LIST

lament	kindle	juncture	gullible	tumult

SET TWO

6. "I am miserable today. My dog died last night, and I've had him since I was eight." What is the person going to do about the dog's death? _____

7. "My life is in an uproar since three of my teenage cousins have come to visit." What state is the person's life in? _____

8. "Seeing the movie set in Kenya awakened an interest in me to travel there." What did the film do to the person? _____

9. "The wall is starting to swell at the point in the kitchen where the panels meet; it looks like they were not joined well." In what area has a problem developed? _____

10. "I can't believe I wore my pajamas to the party. I didn't realize you were joking when you said to. Why am I so easy to fool?" What kind of person is the speaker? _____

© 2007 Pearson Education, Inc.

Imagine that you write fortunes for cookies. Finish the fortunes using at least five of the vocabulary words.

Beware a stranger who _____
_____

A trip to a foreign country will _____
_____

Look to a friend for _____
_____

A new job will create _____
_____

Your current behavior makes people
think _____

HINT

Watch Your Body Clock

Determining the time of day that you are most productive will make your study time more efficient. Ask yourself whether you are a morning, afternoon, or night person. Don't try to get up early and study if you won't really be awake at that time. Or don't stay up late trying to read if all you want to do is close your eyes. Discover how your body works by paying attention to the times of the day when you feel the most tired and the most alert. Your study time will be improved if you pay attention to your body clock.

▌▌▐▌ WORD LIST

apparent
[ə par′ ənt, ə pâr′-]

adj. easily seen or understood; clear; evident

beguile
[bi gīl′]

v. to charm; to entice; to mislead

gullible
[gul′ ə bəl]

adj. easily fooled; believing

intimate
[in′ tə mit]

adj. of a close, personal, or private nature

juncture
[jungk′ chər]

*n.*1. a stage; a point in time; a moment
2. the point where two items join

kindle
[kin′ dl]

v. 1. to excite; to awaken; to inspire
2. to set fire

lament
[lə ment′]

v. to express grief

passionate
[pash′ ən it]

adj. having strong emotions; enthusiastic; loving

shrewdness
[shrood′ nis]

n. intelligence; common sense

tumult
[too′ mult]

n. uproar; disorder

▌▌▐▌ WORDS TO WATCH

Which words would you like to practice with a bit more? Pick 3–5 words to study and list them below. Write the word, its definition, and compose your own sentence using the word correctly. This extra practice could be the final touch to learning a word.

Word	Definition	Your Sentence
1. _____	_____	_____
2. _____	_____	_____
3. _____	_____	_____
4. _____	_____	_____
5. _____	_____	_____

© 2007 Pearson Education, Inc.

19 Friendship

Many Thanks

Dear Lee,

Thank you for the house-warming gift. The clock is remarkable; it is perfect for my den. I also want to thank you for being so **supportive** over the years. You have kept my secrets **confidential** and given your **sympathy**
5   when I have been upset. You are a person whose **advice** I can trust. What you suggest I do almost always works out. I like to **assume** that I have been a good friend too. I hope I have not **neglected** you these last few months while I have been busy purchasing the house.

Unfortunately, we have had to put up with some **malicious** people over
10   the years (remember Terri from high school—she really tried to destroy our friendship), but we have come through it all. We learned how to **compromise** on that car trip across the United States. I don't regret turning down my music at night so you could get to sleep, and I thank you for letting me stop at every tacky tourist shop even though that wasn't your favorite thing to do.
15   Over the years we have really had the chance to **empathize** with each other as we have faced romantic setbacks, family disasters, and personal problems. I appreciate your going through everything with me. If there were ever a **rift** in our relationship, I don't know what I would do.

Now that I'm settled, I want you to visit often. Enclosed is a picture of the
20   house, so you'll recognize it. Can you make it for dinner next week? I'll call you!

Thanks,
Pat

▌▌▌ PREDICTING

For each set, write the definition on the line next to the word to which it belongs. If you are unsure, return to the reading on page 116, and underline any context clues you find. After you've made your predictions, check your answers against the Word List on page 121. Place a checkmark in the box next to each word whose definition you missed. These are the words you'll want to study closely.

SET ONE

an opinion on how to act	secret	helpful	to suppose	a feeling of tenderness or sorrow

❑ 1. **supportive** (line 3) _____

❑ 2. **confidential** (line 4) _____

❑ 3. **sympathy** (line 4) _____

❑ 4. **advice** (line 5) _____

❑ 5. **assume** (line 6) _____

SET TWO

a break	overlooked	showing a desire to harm another	to understand a person's feelings
to settle a difference by working together			

❑   6. **neglected** (line 7) _____

❑   7. **malicious** (line 9) _____

❑   8. **compromise** (line 11) _____

❑   9. **empathize** (line 15) _____

❑ 10. **rift** (line 17) _____

▌▌▌ SELF-TESTS

1 For each set, match the sentence to the kind of comment it best demonstrates. Use each type once.

SET ONE

KIND OF COMMENT

giving empathy	poor advice	malicious	supportive	assuming something

1. "Oh, I had always believed Anita was married." _____

2. "I'm sorry to hear about your mother's death. I understand how you feel; my mother passed away last month." _____

3. "I recommend that you don't do any work for a week; then maybe they'll appreciate you!" _____

4. "Henry is always so perfect. I can't take it anymore. The boss is going to have to hear something bad about him." _____

5. "You'll be great at the concert; you're an excellent pianist." _____

© 2007 Pearson Education, Inc.

KIND OF COMMENT

confidential   giving sympathy   could lead to neglect   could cause a rift   suggesting a compromise

6. "I'm sorry everyone laughed at you when you asked that question. I didn't think it was dumb." _____

7. "There are several sporting events I want to watch on television, so I might not be able to pay much attention to you this weekend." _____

8. "I'll get up first in the morning to take a shower if you turn down the volume on the television at night." _____

9. "I'm going to quit this job, but it's still a secret, so don't tell anyone!" _____

10. "Iris and Leo are fighting again. Their relationship is in trouble. I'm not trying to split them up, but I'll let his ex-girlfriend know because I heard she wants to get back together with him." _____

2 For Set One match each word with its synonym. For Set Two match each word with its antonym.

SYNONYMS
SET ONE

_____ 1. compromise   a. believe

_____ 2. rift   b. adjust

_____ 3. advice   c. identify

_____ 4. empathize   d. split

_____ 5. assume   e. suggestion

ANTONYMS
SET TWO

_____ 6. malicious   f. open

_____ 7. confidential   g. care

_____ 8. supportive   h. cruelty

_____ 9. neglect   i. kind

_____ 10. sympathy   j. discouraging

3 Use the vocabulary words to complete the following analogies. For instructions see Completing Analogies on page 5. Use each word once.

VOCABULARY LIST

compromise	assume	neglect	confidential	rift
advice	sympathy	supportive	malicious	empathize

1. cold : hot :: union : _____
2. strong wind : downed power lines :: _____ : overgrown garden
3. contact : touch :: loyalty : _____
4. snow : white :: a code : _____
5. write : a form :: _____ : more responsibilities at work
6. angry : slow waiter :: _____ : a friend running for office
7. open a book : read :: meet a friend also going through a divorce : _____
8. simple : complex :: _____ : disagree
9. taxi driver : ride :: counselor : _____
10. bashful : shy :: mean : _____

4 Circle the word that best completes each sentence.

1. I will (assume, neglect) office as president of the club in January.
2. The (advice, rift) in our friendship occurred over a silly disagreement.
3. The letter was supposed to be (malicious, confidential), but somehow everyone in the office found out about its contents.
4. I didn't (neglect, empathize) my studies because I wanted to do well in the class.
5. I listened to the instructor's (sympathy, advice) and studied every night.
6. I thought Julio liked Wanda, but he made some (malicious, supportive) comments about her at lunch today.
7. By learning to (assume, compromise) my husband and I have enjoyed thirty years of marriage.
8. I showed my (rift, sympathy) for Jane's lost dog by sending her a card.
9. My coach has been especially (confidential, supportive) this semester; she has helped me through several personal problems.
10. I (empathize, compromise) with Lori; I too had a hard time adjusting to college.

© 2007 Pearson Education, Inc.

Pretend you are Lee and write Pat back. Use at least seven vocabulary words in your response.

Dear Pat,

_____

_____

_____

_____

_____

_____

_____

_____

_____

_____

Sincerely,
Lee

HINT

Outlining

When writing, it helps to make an outline of your ideas. You can always change the outline if you get better ideas, but it is a good way to help you get organized at the beginning of a writing project.

Informal Outline
Write your thesis (your main point) at the top of the paper. In a few key words, list the three or more points you want to cover.

1. _____

2. _____

3. _____

Look at the order in which you listed your points. Is there a reason to list them that way? Some possible methods of arrangement:

- Chronological (by time)
- From the least- to the most-important point
- From the most- to the least-important point
- A problem and its solution

Rearrange your points if you need to.

Now you will have an easier time as you start writing, and you won't forget an important point that you wanted to make.

▌▌▐▌ WORD LIST

advice
[ad vīs′]
n. an opinion on how to act; a recommendation

assume
[ə soom′]
v. 1. to suppose; to believe
2. to take on

compromise
[kom′ prə mīz]
v. to settle a difference by working together and modifying one's demands

confidential
[kän′ fə den′ chəl]
adj. spoken or written for only a few people to know about; secret

empathize
[em′ pə thīz]
v. to identify with another person's situation; to understand a person's feelings

malicious
[mə lish′ əs]
adj. feeling or showing a desire to harm another; hateful; mean

neglect
[ni glekt′]
v. to overlook; to fail to pay attention to

rift
[rift]
n. a break; division; split

supportive
[sə pôr′ tiv]
adj. giving strength and encouragement; helpful

sympathy
[sim′ pə thē]
n. 1. a feeling of tenderness or sorrow for another person's pain
2. a feeling of loyalty

▌▌▐▌ WORDS TO WATCH

Which words would you like to practice with a bit more? Pick 3–5 words to study and list them below. Write the word, its definition, and compose your own sentence using the word correctly. This extra practice could be the final touch to learning a word.

Word	Definition	Your Sentence
1. _____	_____	_____
2. _____	_____	_____
3. _____	_____	_____
4. _____	_____	_____
5. _____	_____	_____

© 2007 Pearson Education, Inc.

20 Romance

The Flirting Seminar

Thank you all for coming this evening. My name is Emma Mansfield. Look around and you'll see men and women of all ages and backgrounds. Some of you are divorced, others are widowed, and 5 others never married. But you all have something in common. You want to find a better way to **relate** to other people. First of all, I want to **clarify** something: there is nothing wrong with a little 10 flirting. Some of you may think flirting will make you look pushy or **manipulative.** But flirting is a harmless way to get to know other people. It doesn't cost a thing, you can do it 15 anywhere and any time, and it's fun!

Let's take an example. On a normal day you will complete simple tasks at the grocery, the post office, and so on. In each of these places, you have the opportunity to interact with people. What better way to practice the flirting 20 techniques I'm going to give you? The rest of the evening I'm going to **disclose** the secrets behind successful flirting.

Look at the screen for a few basics to begin with.

1. Dress to **impress.** Always look your best. You never know who you'll run into. 25

2. **Establish** eye contact. Get the person to look at you. And smile.

3. Show **genuine** interest. Let him or her know that you're really interested.

You see, you never know when or where you're going to meet someone that you find attractive. If you make these techniques part of your everyday life, you'll be ready to enter the **uncharted** world of romance. People never know 30 what they will find! If you pay close attention to the rest of the seminar I can **ensure** that you won't feel **intimidated;** you will be able to flirt with confidence in the future.

For each set, write the definition on the line next to the word to which it belongs. If you are unsure, return to the reading on page 122, and underline any context clues you find. After you've made your predictions, check your answers against the Word List on page 127. Place a checkmark in the box next to each word whose definition you missed. These are the words you'll want to study closely.

SET ONE

to interest	controlling	to make clear	to make public	to connect

❑ 1. **relate** (line 8) _____

❑ 2. **clarify** (line 9) _____

❑ 3. **manipulative** (line 13) _____

❑ 4. **disclose** (line 21) _____

❑ 5. **impress** (line 24) _____

SET TWO

real	to make certain	to form	scared	unexplored

❑ 6. **establish** (line 26) _____

❑ 7. **genuine** (line 27) _____

❑ 8. **uncharted** (line 30) _____

❑ 9. **ensure** (line 32) _____

❑ 10. **intimidated** (line 32) _____

▌▌▊▌ SELF-TESTS

1 Circle the correct meaning of each vocabulary word.

1. **relate:**	keep back	tell
2. **ensure:**	make certain	doubt
3. **manipulative:**	freeing	controlling
4. **establish:**	form	destroy
5. **intimidated:**	scared	brave
6. **genuine:**	fake	real
7. **impress:**	interest	bore

© 2007 Pearson Education, Inc.

8. **clarify:**   confuse   make clear

9. **uncharted:**   known   unexplored

10. **disclose:**   make public   hide

2 Complete the reading using the vocabulary words from the list below. Use each word once.

VOCABULARY LIST

ensure	relate	disclose	uncharted	impress
established	genuine	clarify	intimidated	manipulative

"Hello, Chris? It's Louie. You won't believe it but last night I went to a seminar on flirting. Why? Because I want to date more and you know how it is sometimes—you see an attractive woman, and you don't know what to do or say. Well, sometimes I feel (1)_____. I don't suppose you know what that's like. Emma Mansfield told us what to do. She said she could (2)_____ we would meet people if we followed her advice. She said flirting isn't about being pushy or (3)_____. She really helped to (4)_____ some of the basics last night. She said you've got to remember three things. You should dress to (5)_____. Well, at least be clean and have your hair combed! Ha, ha! And try to get the person to look at you. What? Oh, there were women there—lots of them. People of all ages. There was one who was gorgeous. Did I talk to her? No, but I looked at her and she looked at me. You could say we (6)_____ eye contact. Why not? Well, we didn't learn what to say this time. Emma is going to (7)_____ that information in session two on how to talk to someone you like. Do you want to go with me next week? Come on, be a (8)_____ friend and go. Maybe we can practice together. Yeah, you help me (9)_____ to women, and I'll help you understand the man's points of view. Remember, our futures are (10)_____; we should have fun while we explore them. Is it a deal? Okay, Christina, see you later. Bye."

3 Put a T for true or F for false next to each statement according to the comments made by Emma Mansfield, the speaker on page 122.

_____ 1. Flirting is usually manipulative.

_____ 2. Emma ensured the crowd that they could meet new people while doing daily tasks.

_____ 3. According to Emma, you will be able to better navigate the uncharted world of love with her advice.

_____ 4. A lot of people at Emma's seminars feel too intimidated to flirt.

_____ 5. Establishing eye contact isn't important to Emma's rules of flirting.

_____ 6. The right kind of clothes can help you impress someone.

_____ 7. In Emma's seminar, she is going to disclose how to make more money.

_____ 8. Never show genuine interest; you may look pushy.

_____ 9. According to Emma, relating to someone is easier if you know her techniques.

_____ 10. Emma clarified that flirting was harmless.

4 Complete the sentences using the word list below. Use each word once.

VOCABULARY LIST

relate	intimidated	genuine	clarify	ensure
manipulated	uncharted	disclosed	impressed	established

1. Most of the planets in our solar system are _____.

2. I was _____ by the invitation to Scarlett's party; it sounded like a very formal occasion.

3. I _____ myself by getting a perfect score on the test.

4. To _____ the time of the meeting, I called the secretary.

5. At a special meeting yesterday, the government _____ the contents of files that had been sealed for forty years.

6. I asked Grandpa to _____ the story about the time he got lost in a cave.

7. I _____ an exercise regimen to get back in shape.

8. The mother showed _____ love for her baby.

9. Carol _____ the place cards at the dinner table so she was sitting next to Bill.

10. To _____ success on the test, I studied all weekend and reread parts of the textbook.

© 2007 Pearson Education, Inc.

Create a simple drawing that illustrates two or three of the vocabulary words, or bring a picture from a magazine that could illustrate a few of the words and tape it to this page (or to a piece of paper). Write a brief story to accompany the drawing or picture that uses the words. Be prepared to share your picture and story in class.

Story: _____

_____

_____

_____

_____

_____

_____

_____

HINT

Play with Words

To make reading and vocabulary fun, learn to enjoy using words in recreational contexts.

- Pick up the newspaper and do the crossword puzzle.
- Buy popular board games that are based on using words—for example, Scrabble, Boggle, or Scattergories. Invite your friends over to play.
- Play simple word games when traveling—for example, the first person says a word with at least five letters, and the next person must say a word that begins with the last letter of the previous word: *silent, temperature, easier, random.*
- Write cards, letters, or e-mail messages that play with language—for example, write a thank-you note that uses several synonyms to express what a "fun" time you had at a friend's house or party: *delightful, entertaining, amusing, pleasurable.* Your friends will enjoy getting your letters or e-mail.

▌▌▐ WORD LIST

clarify
[klâr′ ə fī]
v. to make clear; to explain

disclose
[dis klōz′]
v. to make public

ensure
[en shûr′, -shoor′]
v. to make certain

establish
[e stab′ lish]
v. to form; to make

genuine
[jen′ yo͞o in]
adj. real; true

impress
[im pres′]
v. to influence; to interest

intimidated
[in tim′ i dā təd]
adj. scared; frightened

manipulative
[mə nip′ yə lā′ tiv, -lə tiv]
adj. using for one's own purposes; controlling

relate
[rē lāt′]
v. 1. to connect
2. to tell or report

uncharted
[un chär′ təd]
adj. unexplored

▌▌▐ WORDS TO WATCH

Which words would you like to practice with a bit more? Pick 3–5 words to study and list them below. Write the word, its definition, and compose your own sentence using the word correctly. This extra practice could be the final touch to learning a word.

Word	Definition	Your Sentence
1. _____	_____	_____
2. _____	_____	_____
3. _____	_____	_____
4. _____	_____	_____
5. _____	_____	_____

© 2007 Pearson Education, Inc.

21 Word Parts III

Look for words with these **prefixes**, **roots**, and/or **suffixes** as you work through this book. You may have already seen some of them, and you will see others in later chapters. Learning basic word parts can help you figure out the meaning of unfamiliar words.

prefix: a word part added to the beginning of a word that changes the meaning of the root

root: a word's basic part with its essential meaning

suffix: a word part added to the end of a word; indicates the part of speech

WORD PART	MEANING	EXAMPLES AND DEFINITIONS
Prefixes		
col-, con-	together, with	*collaborative:* working together *context:* a situation; involved with other elements
re-	again, back	*review:* to look at something again *reflect:* to look back on
un-	not	*uncharted:* not charted or mapped *unwanted:* not wanted or desired
Roots		
-pas-, -pat-, -path-	feeling, disease	*sympathy:* a feeling of tenderness for someone's pain *psychopath:* a person with a disease of the mind
-que-, -qui-	to seek, to ask	*request:* to seek permission *acquire:* to get something
-spect-	look at	*inspection:* the act of looking into something *spectator:* someone who looks at something
-vid-, -vis-	see	*evident:* clearly seen *television:* a device for viewing images
Suffixes		
-ate, -ize (makes a verb)	to make	*anticipate:* to wait for; to look forward to *empathize:* to be understanding of
-al, -ic (makes an adjective)	relating to	*musical:* relating to music *thematic:* relating to a theme or topic
-ose, -ous (makes an adjective)	full of	*morose:* full of sadness *monotonous:* full of monotony; boring

1 Read each definition and choose the appropriate word from the list below. Use each word once. The meaning of the word part is underlined to help you make the connection. Refer to the Word Part list if you need help.

VOCABULARY LIST

passionate	evident	collaborate	inspect	relate
courageous	memorize	chronological	inquisitive	uninformed

1. to work <u>together</u> _____

2. to tell <u>again</u> _____

3. to <u>feel</u> strongly about _____

4. <u>full of courage</u> _____

5. <u>relating to time</u> order _____

6. to <u>make</u> part of memory _____

7. to <u>look</u> into something _____

8. plainly <u>seen</u> _____

9. <u>not</u> knowledgeable _____

10. <u>seeking</u> information _____

2 Finish the sentences with the meaning of each word part from the list below. Use each meaning once. The word part is underlined to help you make the connection.

VOCABULARY LIST

look at	full of	disease	related to	with
to seek	not	to make	see	again

1. Because the in<u>vis</u>ible man was impossible to _____, he could overhear a lot of gossip about himself.

2. I am going to re<u>quest</u> tomorrow off from work. When I go _____ my boss's approval, I will tell him how important it is that I go skiing.

3. If you <u>re</u>peat a class, you have to take it _____.

4. A psycho<u>path</u> is a person with a mental _____.

5. Something comi<u>cal</u> is _____ comedy.

6. Because Tina is <u>con</u>genial, people like to work _____ her.

7. The wedding was a joy<u>ous</u> occasion; it was _____ happiness.

8. The house was <u>un</u>usual because it did _____ have a front door.

9. I need to put on my <u>spect</u>acles to _____ the newspaper.

10. I fanta<u>size</u> about being a famous pianist; _____ my dream come true I need to spend more time practicing.

© 2007 Pearson Education, Inc.

3 Finish the story using the word parts below. Use each word part once. Your knowledge of word parts, as well as the context clues, will help you create the correct words. If you do not understand the meaning of a word you have made, check the dictionary for the definition or to see whether the word exists.

VOCABULARY PARTS

con	vis	al	ate	ous
qui	spect	un	re	path

THE SEARCH

Tony and Lena were looking for an inexpensive apartment to rent. Neither of them had jobs that provided much money. They in<u>(1)</u>_____red about availability at one place and were told to come see it. The place was <u>(2)</u>_____acular. The complex had a pool, a recreation area, and a laundry room. The bedrooms were so large they could easily accommod<u>(3)</u>_____ four people and the kitchen was recently remodeled. However, they were <u>(4)</u>_____able to work it into their budgets. They had to be very economic<u>(5)</u>_____.

 They thought the chance of finding a two-bedroom apartment within their price range was impossible. Their friends sym<u>(6)</u>_____ized with them, and said they would keep their eyes open. Then Pam called and said she knew how she could <u>(7)</u>_____nect them with a good deal. She had just seen an ad on tele<u>(8)</u>_____ion for apartments. The apartments were supposed to be affordable. They called the number and went to visit the place. The grounds and the apartment were wondr<u>(9)</u>_____. They could not <u>(10)</u>_____sist renting there. Their happiness was now complete.

4 Pick the best definition for each underlined word from the list below using your knowledge of word parts. Circle the word part in each of the underlined words.

a. to make a judgment

b. look into one's feelings

c. view

d. full of offense; disgraceful

e. overcome

f. have similar feelings

g. relating to drama

h. come together with force

i. to make new again

j. not good; regrettably

_____ 1. The vista of the lake from the path among the elms looked inviting.

_____ 2. My latest conquest was Mount Whitney. Now I have climbed every peak in the state.

_____ 3. After some introspection, Alexa knew which job would be the best for her.

_____ 4. I should not always criticize my brother; sometimes I need to say something nice.

_____ 5. Unfortunately I forgot to bring spoons, so we will have to eat our ice cream with forks.

_____ 6. The student's dramatic presentation caused the class to weep.

_____ 7. I have to renew my library card; I haven't used it in four years.

_____ 8. My new roommate and I are compatible; we both like the same things.

_____ 9. If a space shuttle and a planet collide, there will be a huge mess.

_____ 10. Her low-cut dress was outrageous; it was not at all appropriate for a family gathering.

5 A good way to remember word parts is to pick one word that uses a word part and understand how that word part functions in the word. Then you can apply that meaning to other words that have the same word part. Use the words to help you match the word part to its meaning.

SET ONE

_____ 1. col-, con-: collaborative, context, congenial

_____ 2. -que-, -qui-: request, acquire, exquisite

_____ 3. -al, -ic: vital, philosophical, phonics

_____ 4. un-: unbridled, uncharted, uncertain

_____ 5. -spect-: inspect, aspect, spectator

a. look at

b. not

c. to seek, to ask

d. together, with

e. relating to

SET TWO

_____ 6. re-: repeat, retain, reflect

_____ 7. -ate, -ize: passionate, procrastinate, prioritize

_____ 8. -pas-, -pat-, -path-: passionate, sympathy, psychopath

_____ 9. -vid-, -vis-: evident, visible, visionary

_____ 10. -ose, -ous,: morose, monotonous, villainous

f. feeling, disease

g. to make

h. full of

i. again, back

j. see

© 2007 Pearson Education, Inc.

When you read for fun, it can be counterproductive to stop and look up every word you don't know—you will become frustrated with reading instead of enjoying it. As this book advocates, looking for context clues is the best way to find the meaning of an unknown word, but sometimes this method doesn't work. There are ways of keeping track of unfamiliar words; try these methods to see which fits your style.

- Keep a piece of paper and a pen next to you and write down the word and page number.
- Keep a piece of paper next to you and rip it into small pieces or use sticky notes. Put a piece between the pages where the word you don't know is located. For added help, write the word on the paper.
- If the book belongs to you, circle the words you don't know and flip through the book later to find them.
- If the book belongs to you, dog-ear the page (turn the corner down) where the word you don't know is located. This method is useful when you don't have a pen or paper.
- Repeat the word and page number to yourself a few times. Try to connect the page number to a date to help you remember it.

When you are done reading for the day, get your dictionary and look up the words you marked. The last two methods work best if you don't read many pages before you look up the words or if there are only a few words you don't know. Using these methods will help you learn new words without destroying the fun of reading. Note: If you come across a word you don't know several times and not knowing its meaning keeps you from understanding what is going on, then it's a good idea to stop and look up the word.

INTERACTIVE EXERCISE

Use the dictionary to find a word you don't know that uses the word part listed below. Write the meaning of the word part, the word, and the definition. If your dictionary has the etymology (history) of the word, see how the word part relates to the meaning, and write the etymology after the definition.

Word Part	Meaning	Word	Definition and Etymology
EXAMPLE:			
vid	see	videlicet	that is. Used to introduce examples or lists.
			Latin vidélicet, it is easy to see; vidére, to
			see + licet, it is permitted
1. *con-*			

Word Part	Meaning	Word	Definition and Etymology

2. *pat-* or *path-* _____

_____

_____

_____

3. *re-* _____

_____

_____

_____

4. *spect-* _____

_____

_____

_____

5. *un-* _____

_____

_____

_____

▮▮▮▮ WHERE DID IT COME FROM?

Genuine (Chapter 20): comes from the Latin *genuinus* meaning "natural or native." The word is formed from *genu-* "native" plus *-inus* or -ine "pertaining to." The root is *gignere* meaning "bring into being, birth." The history of the word may also come from the root *genu-* "knee" plus *-inus* or -ine "pertaining to." There was an ancient custom of a father placing a baby on his knees to show that he accepted the child as his. Both etymologies relate to today's meaning of "real or true."

Harbinger (Chapter 24): comes from the German *herbergier* "to shelter." It combines *heri* "army" plus *berga* "shelter." A harbinger was a person who went ahead to find lodgings for an army. It came to apply to any "person or thing that announces the approach of another."

© 2007 Pearson Education, Inc.

22 Cleopatra (69–30 B.C.)

For Love and Power*

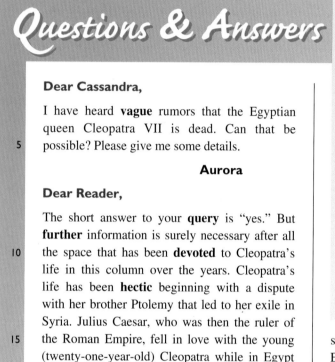

Questions & Answers

Dear Cassandra,

I have heard **vague** rumors that the Egyptian queen Cleopatra VII is dead. Can that be
5 possible? Please give me some details.

Aurora

Dear Reader,

The short answer to your **query** is "yes." But **further** information is surely necessary after all
10 the space that has been **devoted** to Cleopatra's life in this column over the years. Cleopatra's life has been **hectic** beginning with a dispute with her brother Ptolemy that led to her exile in Syria. Julius Caesar, who was then the ruler of
15 the Roman Empire, fell in love with the young (twenty-one-year-old) Cleopatra while in Egypt following his defeat of Pompey. Caesar spent almost a year in Egypt helping Cleopatra regain her title. Their **bliss** was short lived as Cleopatra
20 was forced to marry her eleven-year-old brother as Egyptian tradition demands; Caesar also had much to accomplish back in Rome. Caesar, as we know, was murdered on his return, ending the couple's short romance.

25 Mark Antony, ruler of the Eastern Roman Empire, met Cleopatra a few years after Caesar's death. Cleopatra's **ample** charms—beauty, intelligence, and wit—captured his heart also. Antony enjoyed a **lavish** life style in Egypt.
30 Egyptian rulers are regarded as divine and are well taken care of. Antony reportedly carried a golden scepter and wore a crown. Now for the big problem—Antony was married to Octavian's

"When she heard that he was going to take her back to Rome as a slave, she killed herself."

sister. Octavian, ruler of the Western Roman Empire, became **livid** over Antony's betrayal of 35 his sister. He persuaded the Roman Senate to declare war on Antony and Cleopatra. Antony's and Cleopatra's ships were defeated at the Battle of Actium. In the retreat, Antony was told that Cleopatra was dead, and he killed himself rather 40 than live without her. (A reminder, readers, that true love can exist!) The news, however, was **inaccurate**. Cleopatra was very much alive, and supposedly trying to get Octavian to fall in love with her. She failed. When she heard that he was 45 going to take her back to Rome as a slave, she killed herself. I have heard that she took poison or that she let an asp bite her. Either way, the life of one of the most fascinating women of our era has come to a sad end. This writer will surely 50 miss her.

*Note: The letters are fictitious.

▌▌▐▌ PREDICTING

For each set, write the definition on the line next to the word to which it belongs. If you are unsure, return to the reading on page 134, and underline any context clues you find. After you've made your predictions, check your answers against the Word List on page 139. Place a checkmark in the box next to each word whose definition you missed. These are the words you'll want to study closely.

SET ONE

a question	gave time or attention to	uncertain	busy	more

❑ 1. **vague** (line 3) _____

❑ 2. **query** (line 8) _____

❑ 3. **further** (line 9) _____

❑ 4. **devoted** (line 10) _____

❑ 5. **hectic** (line 12) _____

SET TWO

mistaken	plentiful	absolute joy	furious	extravagant

❑ 6. **bliss** (line 19) _____

❑ 7. **ample** (line 27) _____

❑ 8. **lavish** (line 29) _____

❑ 9. **livid** (line 35) _____

❑ 10. **inaccurate** (line 43) _____

▌▌▐▌ SELF-TESTS

1 In Set One match each term with its synonym. In Set Two match each term with its antonym.

SYNONYMS

SET ONE

_____ 1. lavish   a. incorrect

_____ 2. inaccurate   b. ask

_____ 3. devote   c. abundant

_____ 4. livid   d. promise

_____ 5. query   e. furious

ANTONYMS

_____	6. ample	f. less	
_____	7. hectic	g. sorrow	
_____	8. bliss	h. insufficient	
_____	9. vague	i. relaxed	
_____	10. further	j. sure	

2 Answer each question with the appropriate vocabulary word. Use each word once.

SET ONE

VOCABULARY LIST

ample	bliss	vague	query	hectic

1. What is "Do you like chocolate?" an example of? _____
2. What would directions that don't say whether to turn left or right at a T-intersection probably be called? _____
3. What would a person feel sipping an ice-cold drink on a hot day? _____
4. What would most people consider twelve pizzas for two people? _____
5. How would people likely describe an airport during the Thanksgiving holiday? _____

SET TWO

VOCABULARY LIST

lavish	devoting	inaccurate	further	livid

6. What would you be doing with your time if you volunteered three hours a week at a community center? _____
7. What would a check written yesterday but dated 1995 be called? _____
8. What would your reaction likely be if you found your car bumper smashed? _____
9. What would Fern be doing for Darwin's career if she recommended him as an excellent candidate for the vice-president position at the company? _____
10. What would most people call a sports car as a present? _____

3 Circle the word that correctly completes each sentence.

1. My mother was (hectic, livid) when I came home four hours late.

2. I wanted to (devote, further) more of my time to my schooling, so I am working six hours less this semester.

3. My (bliss, query) was destroyed when a water pipe broke, and I had to spend the day fixing it instead of relaxing on the porch with a good book.

4. My professor said there had been (vague, ample) time to get the project done, so he would not take late work.

5. I didn't understand why the hotel sent me their summer rates when my (query, bliss) had been about availability in the winter.

6. Because the weather reports had been (lavish, inaccurate) all week, I was uncertain about having my party outside on Saturday.

7. I had a (vague, further) feeling that I had forgotten something. When I got home to a wet floor, I realized I hadn't turned the bathtub off.

8. For my birthday my husband (lavished, devoted) gifts on me from opera tickets to a diamond necklace.

9. With two children under five, my sister finds most of her days to be (ample, hectic).

10. To get (further, livid) information on the company, I checked out their Web site.

4 The following are lines from fictitious letters between Cleopatra, Julius Caesar, and Mark Antony. Match each sentence to the word it best fits. Context clues are underlined to help you. Use each word once.

VOCABULARY LIST

further	lavish	vague	inaccurate	devote
bliss	hectic	query	livid	ample

1. You've had <u>plenty</u> of time in Rome, Julius Caesar. Come back to Egypt now if you love me. _____

2. I am sorry Cleopatra, but life is <u>busy</u> in Rome. There are several political problems brewing that I must work to stop. _____

3. Julius Caesar, I am <u>furious</u> with you! Return now or we are through! _____

4. Cleopatra, I will return as soon as I can, and I <u>promise</u> to give you all my <u>time</u>. _____

5. Cleopatra, your <u>generous</u> hospitality has made me feel so welcome. I know I belong in Egypt. _____

6. Mark Antony, when I am with you my days are filled with <u>joy</u>. _____

7. Cleopatra, what <u>more</u> can I do to prove that I love you? _____

8. Mark Antony, your feelings seem <u>uncertain</u>. Why have you married Octavius' sister when you say you love me? _____

9. Cleopatra, I have one <u>question</u>: Do you really love me? _____

10. Anthony, don't listen to stories that I am dead. They are a <u>mistake</u>. I am alive, and I miss you. _____

© 2007 Pearson Education, Inc.

List two examples for each question.

When might someone want to be vague?

1. _____

2. _____

When would one make a query?

1. _____

2. _____

When is further information important?

1. _____

2. _____

What is it easy to be inaccurate about?

1. _____

2. _____

What would you find at a lavish party?

1. _____

2. _____

What makes life hectic?

1. _____

2. _____

What brings bliss to your life?

1. _____

2. _____

What do you have ample of?

1. _____

2. _____

What makes you livid?

1. _____

2. _____

What activities are you devoted to?

1. _____

2. _____

HINT

Idioms

An idiom is a phrase where the meaning of the words cannot be taken literally; the meaning is something other than what the words would usually mean. For example, if someone says, "I couldn't make it to the party because I had **other fish to fry** that night," it doesn't mean the person had a cookout to go to. The person had some other kind of matter that he or she had to attend to. Using context clues can often help you figure out the meaning of an idiom. There are hundreds of idioms in use in English today, and new idioms are sometimes created. Other languages also have idioms that are similar to ones in English. If you are curious about idioms, look for idiom dictionaries that give the meaning and, when known, the history of an idiom.

Idioms can be a colorful way of expressing one's meaning, but they are also an informal way of communicating, and sometimes they are so overused that they lose their impact. For these reasons students usually want to avoid using idioms in their college papers. Idioms, however, are used in informal writing and in speech. Watch where you find idioms and how you use them yourself.

Can you figure out the meanings of the idioms (in bold) in the following sentences?

After I forgot to pick my mom up at the airport, I was **in deep water.**

Carlos and I got along **right off the bat**; we were planning a trip to Europe after knowing each other for two weeks.

ample [am′ pəl]	*adj.* plentiful; more than enough	**inaccurate** [in ak′ yər it]	*adj.* mistaken; incorrect
bliss [blis]	*n.* absolute joy	**lavish** [lav′ ish]	*adj.* extravagant; abundant; generous *v.* to give or spend in large amounts
devote [di vōt′]	*v.* to promise; to give one's time or attention to	**livid** [liv′ id]	*adj.* 1. extremely angry; furious 2. of an abnormal color due to anger or illness
further [fûr′ THûr]	*adj.* 1. more; additional 2. more distant *v.* to promote; to favor	**query** [kwēr′ ē]	*n.* a question *v.* to question; to ask
hectic [hek′ tik]	*adj.* busy and confused; feverish	**vague** [vāg]	*adj.* uncertain; not clearly expressed

▌▌▌ WORDS TO WATCH

Which words would you like to practice with a bit more? Pick 3–5 words to study and list them below. Write the word, its definition, and compose your own sentence using the word correctly. This extra practice could be the final touch to learning a word.

Word	Definition	Your Sentence
1. _____	_____	_____
	_____	_____
2. _____	_____	_____
	_____	_____
3. _____	_____	_____
	_____	_____
4. _____	_____	_____
	_____	_____
5. _____	_____	_____
	_____	_____

© 2007 Pearson Education, Inc.

From the Liberator's Journal*

November 1815

I am not **invincible**. I have had to flee here to Jamaica since my countrymen who are still loyal to Spain have taken back Caracas. The losses of the last five years have been an **affront** to my pride, but I have the **resolve** to continue. I will help to **secure** the freedom of South America. I want to

5　establish a balance of powers based on the British model of government. My voice will be heard!

July 1825

My **noble** efforts have been rewarded. I have helped to free the upper section of Peru, and it has been renamed Bolivia in my honor. The wars are

10　coming to an end. I can now focus on being the president of Colombia. For the last six years the vice-president has had to keep the country in order. During the **interim**, I have been busy as commander-in-chief of the military, but now I am

15　ready to take over my political responsibilities. I hope there is **adequate** time to get all I want done. My dear wife—I miss you Maria Teresa. Why did you have to die so young? I will never marry again. What would you think of the name

20　the people have given me, El Libertador?

May 1830

The last years have not been good. **Aside** from my failed attempt to create a union among the countries formerly controlled by Spain, I could not satisfy the different sides in Colombia, and I had to become a dictator. The assassination attempt in 1828 terrified me! Finally, resignation was my

25　only choice, and tomorrow I head into exile again. I am sick with tuberculosis and may not live much longer, but I do not want to be **morose**. I know that I helped to free my homeland, and if a monument is ever created to honor me, I hope the people will **inscribe** on it, "A man who fought for freedom; a man who wanted peace."

*Note: The journal entries are fictitious.

For each set, write the definition on the line next to the word to which it belongs. If you are unsure, return to the reading on page 140, and underline any context clues you find. After you've made your predictions, check your answers against the Word List on page 145. Place a checkmark in the box next to each word whose definition you missed. These are the words you'll want to study closely.

SET ONE

to succeed in getting	insult	undefeatable	admirable
determination			

❑ 1. **invincible** (line 2) _____

❑ 2. **affront** (line 3) _____

❑ 3. **resolve** (line 4) _____

❑ 4. **secure** (line 4) _____

❑ 5. **noble** (line 7) _____

SET TWO

enough	miserable	time in between	apart	to write on

❑ 6. **interim** (line 13) _____

❑ 7. **adequate** (line 16) _____

❑ 8. **aside** (line 22) _____

❑ 9. **morose** (line 26) _____

❑ 10. **inscribe** (line 27) _____

▌▌▐▌▌ SELF-TESTS

1 Put a T for true or F for false next to each statement.

_____ 1. Waving at someone and saying "Hi" is usually considered an affront.

_____ 2. Serving as president of an organization until a permanent president can be found is an example of an interim position.

_____ 3. One might inscribe a message on an engagement ring.

_____ 4. Locking your house can help to make it secure.

_____ 5. A week of rain can make some people morose.

_____ 6. A banana is an adequate lunch for most people.

_____ 7. Unsure about what color to paint a room shows resolve.

© 2007 Pearson Education, Inc.

_____ 8. Cheating on a test would be a noble action.

_____ 9. If you were to step aside, you would move away from your current spot.

_____10. Losing ten games in a row would be the record of an invincible team.

2 Complete the sentences by using the vocabulary list below. Use each word once.

VOCABULARY LIST

inscribed	aside	secure	invincible	resolved
noble	affront	interim	morose	adequate

1. We have a(n) _____ supply of food for the party.

2. While you look at shoes, I will spend the _____ trying on clothes.

3. If I were Superman, I would be _____ (except around Kryptonite).

4. Chester seems _____; he is always wearing a frown.

5. I was able to _____ tickets to the sold-out concert.

6. I can't believe the _____. That man just walked up to me and called me ugly.

7. I _____ a note in the book I gave my mother.

8. It was _____ of Martin to help establish peace in the neighborhood again after he was falsely accused of the lawn mower incident.

9. The actor whispered a(n) _____ to the audience.

10. The parties _____ the contract dispute after three months of arguing.

3 In Set One match each term with its synonym. In Set Two match each term with its antonym.

SYNONYMS

SET ONE

_____ 1. adequate   a. safe

_____ 2. aside   b. enough

_____ 3. inscribe   c. apart

_____ 4. secure   d. well-born

_____ 5. noble   e. carve

ANTONYMS

SET TWO

_____ 6. interim   f. cheerful

_____ 7. invincible   g. compliment

_____ 8. resolve   h. permanent

_____ 9. morose   i. hesitate

_____ 10. affront   j. weak

4 Finish the reading using the vocabulary words. Use each word once.

VOCABULARY LIST

noble	interim	adequate	inscribed	morose
aside	secure	affront	resolve	invincible

When I was a child, an old man told me a story about his fighting with Simon Bolivar. He said that one time Bolivar had to leave his troops for a month to take care of business in Columbia. During the (1)_____ the men got restless. When he returned he found them (2)_____ : they had lost heart in their campaign. Bolivar had to restore their (3)_____. He addressed the troops: "The Spaniards actions are a(n) (4)_____ to our pride. All men have a right to freedom. Haven't I provided you all with (5)_____ food and supplies?

(6)_____ from a few lonely nights what have you really suffered? Remember our mission is a(n) (7)_____ one. We are in the right! Are you ready to (8)_____ your freedom?" The men yelled "Si!" They now felt (9)_____. Before they left the next morning, the old man (10)_____ the words, "Gracias, Simon" on a rock nearby. I always wanted to find that rock.

© 2007 Pearson Education, Inc.

Write two journal entries about an experience or event that was important to you. Use at least seven of the vocabulary words in your entries.

Date: _____

_____

_____

_____

_____

_____

Date: _____

_____

_____

_____

_____

_____

HINT

Journal Writing

Keeping a journal can improve your writing, reading, and critical thinking skills. You can also build your vocabulary by using the new words you are learning in your entries. When you take the time to write about your feelings and observations of the world, it allows you to reflect on what is happening in your life and often better deal with problems you encounter. You don't have to write in the journal every day; even writing a few times a week will help develop your skills. The following are a few ideas for your journal: describe the people and experiences that you encounter; look at changes in your life; examine your goals for the future; explore your reactions to a movie you have seen or something you have read (a short story, a newspaper article, a textbook chapter); record your experiences with music, food, sports, travel, or a hobby. There is really no end to the ideas that can be captured in a journal. Don't strain to come up with something to write about; let the ideas flow naturally. Enjoy the writing and exploration process. Remember that the journal is for you, so don't worry about other people's reactions to what you write.

▌▌▌ WORD LIST

adequate
[ad′ i kwit]
    adj. sufficient; satisfactory; enough

affront
[ə frunt′]
    n. an insult
    v. to insult; to confront

aside
[ə sīd′]
    adv. to or on one side; away; apart
    n. words spoken confidentially by an actor to the audience

inscribe
[in skrīb′]
    v. to write or carve on a surface or page

interim
[in′ tər əm]
    n. time in between
    adj. temporary

invincible
[in vin′ sə bəl]
    adj. unconquerable; undefeatable; powerful

morose
[mə rōs′]
    adj. gloomy; miserable; depressed

noble
[nō′ bəl]
    adj. 1. admirable; distinguished; of excellent character
        2. well-born; aristocratic
    n. a nobleman or noblewoman

resolve
[ri zolv′]
    n. determination; a firm decision or plan
    v. 1. to make up one's mind; to decide firmly
        2. to solve or settle, such as an argument

secure
[si kyoor′]
    v. 1. to succeed in getting
        2. to make safe
    adj. safe; reliable

▌▌▌ WORDS TO WATCH

Which words would you like to practice with a bit more? Pick 3–5 words to study and list them below. Write the word, its definition, and compose your own sentence using the word correctly. This extra practice could be the final touch to learning a word.

Word	Definition	Your Sentence
1. _____	_____	_____
2. _____	_____	_____
3. _____	_____	_____
4. _____	_____	_____
5. _____	_____	_____

© 2007 Pearson Education, Inc.

24 Victoria Woodhull (1838–1927)

The First Female Candidate for President*

LETTERS TO THE EDITOR

November 1872

Dear Editor,

I was sorry to
5 read your article
that trumpeted the
failure of Victoria
Woodhull's presi-
dential run. That
10 Woodhull had to end her **historic** bid for
president by spending election night in jail is
a crime. Woodhull was the first female candidate for president of the United States, and
I hope not the last. The **circumstances** sur-
15 rounding her campaign were filled with
unusual troubles. The **genesis** of Mrs. Woodhull's running for the highest office in this
country may have come from her attendance
at the 1869 National Female Suffrage Con-
20 vention, which I also attended. Woodhull has
been a strong promoter of equality for wom-
en. Some of Woodhull's ideas have been
offensive to people such as her support of
free love. Her **claim** that the popular Rever-
25 end Beecher was unfaithful to his wife has
also made several members of the public
irate. The assertions that have appeared in
her paper, *Woodhull and Clafin's Weekly*, on
Beecher's affair with his best friend's wife

are in part what led to her being arrested for 30
sending obscene literature through the mail.
A ridiculous charge! The Beecher family has
been against Woodhull's campaign from the
beginning.

I know Mrs. Woodhull realized that run- 35
ning for president was a difficult task, and
she understood that to win she needed money and public support, both of which she had
at one time. As the first female stockbroker,
Woodhull was not **naive** about financial mat- 40
ters. However, I am sure she did not sense
how cruel some people would be and how
they would set out to ruin her campaign and
her life. I hope Woodhull's disaster is not the
harbinger of more ill-will for women trying 45
to enter politics. Women will no longer re-
main **spectators** in politics; we are ready to
be participants. The public needs to understand that women will not **waver**. We are
moving forward. Women will get the right to 50
vote, and a woman will be president of the
United States some day.

With hope for the future,

Elizabeth Cady Stanton

*Note: The letter is fictitious.

▌▌▌▌ PREDICTING

For each set, write the definition on the line next to the word to which it belongs. If you are unsure, return to the reading on page 146, and underline any context clues you find. After you've made your predictions, check your answers against the Word List on page 151. Place a checkmark in the box next to each word whose definition you missed. These are the words you'll want to study closely.

SET ONE

insulting	beginning	famous in history	a declaration

the conditions around an event

- ☐ 1. **historic** (line 10) _____
- ☐ 2. **circumstances** (line 14) _____
- ☐ 3. **genesis** (line 16) _____
- ☐ 4. **offensive** (line 23) _____
- ☐ 5. **claim** (line 24) _____

SET TWO

people who watch	angry	to hesitate	ignorant

a person or thing that announces the approach of another

- ☐ 6. **irate** (line 27) _____
- ☐ 7. **naive** (line 40) _____
- ☐ 8. **harbinger** (line 45) _____
- ☐ 9. **spectators** (line 47) _____
- ☐ 10. **waver** (line 49) _____

▌▌▌▌ SELF-TESTS

1 For each set, complete the analogies. See Completing Analogies on page 5 for instructions and practice.

SET ONE

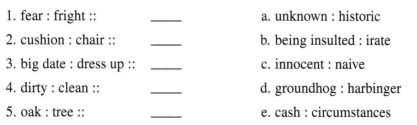

1. fear : fright ::   _____   a. unknown : historic
2. cushion : chair ::   _____   b. being insulted : irate
3. big date : dress up ::   _____   c. innocent : naive
4. dirty : clean ::   _____   d. groundhog : harbinger
5. oak : tree ::   _____   e. cash : circumstances

© 2007 Pearson Education, Inc.

6. firm : solid ::   _____   f. sure : waver

7. ate too much : full ::   _____   g. origin : genesis

8. honey : sweet ::   _____   h. binoculars : spectator

9. nervous : confident ::   _____   i. smell of a skunk : offensive

10. racket : tennis player ::   _____   j. car accident : claim

2 In each group circle the word that does not have a connection to the other three words.

1. claim	declare	assert	deny
2. harbinger	forerunner	harvest	approach
3. irate	calm	angry	enraged
4. simple	experienced	innocent	naive
5. participant	viewer	spectator	observer
6. condition	circumstance	fact	isolation
7. offensive	pleasant	insulting	aggressive
8. genesis	origin	result	start
9. swing	waver	unsure	positive
10. historic	notable	average	famous

3 Match each sentence to the word it illustrates. Context clues are underlined to help you. Look for synonyms, antonyms, examples, or general meaning of a sentence. Use each word once.

VOCABULARY LIST

irate	offensive	historic	spectator	naive

1. "What an amazing throw! I'm so glad I came to see the game." _____
2. "I thought he was polite, but he came up to me and said, "Your haircut is horrible." _____
3. "I've never done this before." _____
4. "I can't believe they made a mistake on my credit card bill again!" _____
5. "This house was built in 1854. It is the oldest structure in town." _____

VOCABULARY LIST

waver	claim	genesis	harbinger	circumstances

6. "My assertion is that I returned the book despite what the library insists." _____

7. "The accident happened on a snowy morning on a deserted road." _____

8. "I hate to hesitate, but now that it is raining I'm not sure I want to go." _____

9. "When the club began, it only had five people, and now it has two hundred." _____

10. "The birds are returning; spring can't be far behind." _____

4 Finish the headlines. Use each word once.

VOCABULARY LIST

offensive	genesis	spectator	naive	harbinger
claims	irate	waver	historic	circumstances

1. _____ **House Up for Sale—Owner Says "George Washington Slept Here!"**

2. Family _____ Force Candidate to Withdraw from Governor's Race

3. _____ of County's Financial Problems Stem from Five-Year-Old Decision

4. New Barbeque Restaurant's Odors Found _____ by Next Door Businesses

5. Presidential Candidate _____ Conspiracy Against Her Campaign

6. Townspeople _____ Over Increased Taxes

7. Several _____ People Fooled by Phone Fraud

8. Is Early Snowfall _____ of a Long Winter?

9. Conservation Group Won't _____ : Historic Barn Must be Saved

10. _____ Falls from Tree While Watching Presidents' Day Parade

© 2007 Pearson Education, Inc.

Pretend you are a journalist covering Woodhull's presidential campaign. Using six of the vocabulary words, write questions you want to ask at her next press conference. You don't need to know the answers to the questions. For example: What would you do, Mrs. Woodhull, if you were president and an irate citizen started yelling at you while you were addressing a meeting?

1. _____

2. _____

3. _____

4. _____

5. _____

6. _____

HINT

Tips for Enjoying Fiction

Readers enjoy a book more when they become involved with it. Try to put yourself in a novel or short story you are reading by imaging yourself in a character's situation. What would you do if you had to stop an alien invasion, cope with a broken heart, or solve a murder? Learn to appreciate the descriptions of the places in the story. Try to visualize yourself hiking through the jungle, cooking a big meal in the kitchen, or hiding under a bed. Look for the author's message as you read. Ask yourself what point the author is trying to get across. Do you agree or disagree with the author's point? By putting yourself in the story and thinking about the significance of events, you will want to keep reading to see what happens to the characters because now they and their world are a part of you.

▎▎▊▊ WORD LIST

circumstance
[sûr′ kəm stans′]
n. 1. a fact or condition around an event (often plural)
2. (plural) one's financial condition

claim
[klām]
n. 1. a declaration or assertion
2. a demand or request
v. 1. to declare; to assert
2. to demand as one's due

genesis
[jen′ ə sis]
n. origin; beginning

harbinger
[här′ bin jər]
n. a person or thing that announces the approach of another; forerunner

historic
[his tôr′ ik]
adj. famous or important in history; notable

irate
[ī rāt′]
adj. angry; enraged; furious

naive or naïve
[nä ēv′]
adj. ignorant; innocent; simple

offensive
[ô fen′ siv, ə fen′ siv]
adj. 1. insulting; disgusting
2. aggressive; attacking
n. aggressive action or attitude

spectator
[spek′ tāt′ ər]
n. a person who watches

waver
[wā′ vər]
v. 1. to be unsure; to hesitate
2. to swing or move back and forth
3. to shake, used of a sound

▎▎▊▊ WORDS TO WATCH

Which words would you like to practice with a bit more? Pick 3–5 words to study and list them below. Write the word, its definition, and compose your own sentence using the word correctly. This extra practice could be the final touch to learning a word.

Word	Definition	Your Sentence
1. _____	_____	_____
2. _____	_____	_____
3. _____	_____	_____
4. _____	_____	_____
5. _____	_____	_____

© 2007 Pearson Education, Inc.

Star Athlete*

Yao Continues to Wow On and Off the Court

As the 2005 NBA season comes to a close, it's time to **reflect** on the remarkable career of Yao Ming, the seven
5 foot, 6 inch center for the Houston Rockets. He has had another successful year finishing the regular season averaging 18.3 points and 8.4
10 rebounds.

Considering how much basketball has become a part of Yao's life, it is surprising that he was not ready to **immerse**
15 himself in the game as a young child in Shanghai. Both his parents are over six feet and played basketball. His mother was captain of China's national women's team and his father played with a local pro club in
20 Shanghai. They both encouraged him to pursue basketball, but he wasn't interested until he was nine. He played in his first organized game when he was ten.

He joined the Shanghai Sharks in 1997 and
25 played with them until he was drafted by Houston as a first-round draft pick in 2002. He has also played for the Chinese national team during the NBA offseason. In 2004 he helped China make it into the top eight teams at the Olympics in Athens. He had
30 vowed not to shave for six months if his team did not make it into the final eight. With Yao's leadership, they succeeded by beating Serbia and Montenegro 67–66. But Yao's constant playing has made him **weary**. This spring he revealed that he was excited
35 about having a summer free from playing and a chance to relax.

For professional athletes it is **inevitable** that critics look at every **aspect** of their playing, and Yao gets no special treatment here. Stamina is **vital** to a
40 top athlete, and Yao continues to tire too easily. As a child, running up and down the courts left him winded, and critics note that endurance is still a problem. Yao's other main difficulty is his lack of aggressiveness. Yao
45 needs to take a more dominant role on the court. On the other hand, Yao has worked on adding upper-body strength to match his lower-body muscle. And a sum-
50 mer off from playing could give Yao the time to work on conditioning.

Enthusiasm for Yao has been **unbridled** in China and in the
55 U.S. Yao fan clubs are popular, and his fans have had plenty of reasons to be **jubilant.** A few of Yao's many accomplishments include NBA All-Rookie First Team honors after averaging 13.5 points with 8.2
60 rebounds in the 2002–03 season, serving as the starting center for the Western Conference in the 2003 NBA All-Star game, and earning the Western Conference Player of the Week honors for March 8, 2004. Off the court, Yao is a Global Ambassador for
65 the Special Olympics. Fan interest also spreads to wanting to know more personal information like his favorite color (blue), food (burgers and his mom's cooking), and hobbies (playing video games, music, and reading).
70

When Yao was picked to carry the flag for China at the 2004 Olympics, one Chinese official mentioned Yao's **integrity** and sense of humor as reasons he was chosen. His teammates also say he is a **congenial** fellow, and he even knows how to joke
75 with the press. At one event, he told journalists that he would love to take each one of them to dinner—as long as their articles were complimentary. Yao's height and basketball skills put him in a different category from a lot of us, but
80 he sounds like the kind of guy this journalist would love to share a burger with.

*Note: The article is fictitious.

For each set, write the definition on the line next to the word to which it belongs. If you are unsure, return to the reading on page 152, and underline any context clues you find. After you've made your predictions, check your answers against the Word List on page 157. Place a checkmark in the box next to each word whose definition you missed. These are the words you'll want to study closely.

SET ONE

tired	part	to think seriously about	unavoidable
to surround			

❑ 1. **reflect** (line 3) _____

❑ 2. **immerse** (line 14) _____

❑ 3. **weary** (line 34) _____

❑ 4. **inevitable** (line 37) _____

❑ 5. **aspect** (line 38) _____

SET TWO

honesty	friendly	free	important	joyful

❑ 6. **vital** (line 39) _____

❑ 7. **unbridled** (line 55) _____

❑ 8. **jubilant** (line 58) _____

❑ 9. **integrity** (line 73) _____

❑ 10. **congenial** (line 75) _____

▌▌▐▌ SELF-TESTS

1 Circle the correct meaning of each vocabulary word.

1. **reflect:**	to think	to act
2. **integrity:**	truthfulness	dishonesty
3. **aspect:**	phase	entire
4. **inevitable:**	unavoidable	preventable
5. **vital:**	unnecessary	essential
6. **weary:**	tired	energetic
7. **immerse:**	to absorb	to withdraw
8. **unbridled:**	free	limited
9. **congenial:**	pleasant	mean
10. **jubilant:**	dejected	joyful

© 2007 Pearson Education, Inc.

2 Finish the sentences using the vocabulary words. Use each word once.

VOCABULARY LIST

unbridled	weary	reflect	jubilant	inevitable
congenial	vital	integrity	aspect	immerse

1. It was _____ that we would have at least one argument on a six-week trip together.

2. This past weekend doesn't _____ my usual behavior; I rarely stay out until three in the morning.

3. His angry _____ warned me not to ask how his team did.

4. The athlete's _____ was refreshing; he had refused to use any kind of drugs his whole career.

5. I chose to live with a family because I wanted to _____ myself in the Spanish language while studying in Mexico.

6. Our hostess is so _____. She said we should help ourselves to anything we wanted to eat in her kitchen.

7. It is _____ that everyone stays with our group; it is easy to get lost in this huge stadium.

8. The crowd was _____ until the announcer said there might be a penalty, and the points wouldn't count.

9. The long speech was beginning to bore the _____ audience.

10. Get up, everyone! My excitement is _____. It's almost six, and we have so much to see!

3 Put a T for true or F for false next to each statement.

_____ 1. If you immerse yourself in your studies you will usually do better in a class.

_____ 2. The way one dresses can reflect one's personality.

_____ 3. Being on time to pick someone up at the airport would show a person's integrity.

_____ 4. Fans would be jubilant about a season if their team lost all its games.

_____ 5. People's excitement can be unbridled when they win on a game show.

_____ 6. Taking tests is an aspect of school that most students enjoy.

_____ 7. Getting a good night's sleep usually makes people feel weary.

_____ 8. It is inevitable that one will step in a puddle each day.

_____ 9. It is vital to eat a big meal before going swimming.

_____10. A congenial person is usually popular at parties.

4 Finish the analogies. See Completing Analogies on page 5 for instructions and practice. Use each word once.

VOCABULARY LIST

weary	reflect	vital	aspects	congenial
inevitable	jubilant	immerse	unbridled	integrity

1. laughter : contagious :: feelings : _____

2. doubt: believe :: _____ : avoidable

3. laugh : a joke :: _____ : a long drive

4. sense of humor : comedian :: _____ : teacher

5. a speeding ticket : mad :: an "A" on a paper : _____

6. sharpen a pencil : write :: turn up the music : _____

7. math or art : majors :: angry or friendly : _____

8. spend 12 hours a day at a job : overworked :: shaking hands : _____

9. query : want an answer :: _____ : buying a house

10. separate : unite :: unimportant : _____

© 2007 Pearson Education, Inc.

Answer the following questions.

1. How would a congenial person act?

   _____

2. What item in your bedroom reflects your interests or hobbies?

   _____

3. What issue do you feel it is vital all people be aware of?

   _____

4. What makes you weary?

   _____

5. What is an inevitable problem for most students?

   _____

6. What are two occupations that seem to lack integrity in recent years?

   _____   _____

7. What activity do you have an unbridled enthusiasm for?

   _____

8. Where would you find jubilant people?

   _____

9. What aspect of college do you like most? Why?

   _____

10. What topic would you like to immerse yourself in?

   _____

HINT

Make Learning Fun

Think about the kinds of activities you like to do and see if you can incorporate the traits involved in those activities to your learning experiences. If you like group activities (team sports, going to big parties) create study groups. If you like to draw, add visual elements to your notes, draw what happens in a story you read, make a diagram to help you understand a concept. The more you enjoy what you do, whether in school or at work, the more you want to do it. Find the ways to make your life and learning fun.

aspect
[as′pekt]

n. 1. a characteristic; a part; a phase
2. appearance to the eye or mind; look
3. an expression or attitude

congenial
[kən jēn′ yəl]

adj. friendly; pleasant; agreeable

immerse
[i mûrs′]

v. to surround; to absorb

inevitable
[in ev′ ə tə bəl]

adj. incapable of being prevented; unavoidable; certain
n. something that is unavoidable

integrity
[in teg′ ri tē]

n. honesty; reliability; truthfulness; honor

jubilant
[jōō′ bə lənt]

adj. joyful; thrilled

reflect
[ri flekt′]

v. 1. to think seriously about
2. to mirror
3. to show as a result of what one does; to signal

unbridled
[un brīd′ dəld]

adj. free; unrestricted; uncontrolled

vital
[vī′ təl]

adj. important; essential

weary
[wēr′ ē]

adj. tired; exhausted
v. to tire; to grow tired

▌▌▌▌ WORDS TO WATCH

Which words would you like to practice with a bit more? Pick 3–5 words to study and list them below. Write the word, its definition, and compose your own sentence using the word correctly. This extra practice could be the final touch to learning a word.

Word	Definition	Your Sentence
1. _____	_____	_____
_____		_____
2. _____	_____	_____
_____		_____
3. _____	_____	_____
_____		_____
4. _____	_____	_____
_____		_____
5. _____	_____	_____
_____		_____

© 2007 Pearson Education, Inc.

26 Review

Focus on Chapters 18–25

The following activities give you a chance to interact some more with the vocabulary words you've been learning. By looking at art, taking tests, answering questions, doing a crossword puzzle, and acting, you will see which words you know well and which you still need to work with.

1. _____

2. _____

3. _____

4. _____

5. _____

6. _____

7. _____

8. _____

9. _____

10. _____

11. _____

12. _____

Match each picture on page 158 with one of the following vocabulary words. Use each word once.

VOCABULARY LIST

confidential	kindle	livid	immerse
noble	spectator	intimidate	supportive
historic	lament	weary	inscribe

▌▌▌▌ SELF-TESTS

1 Pick the word that best completes the sentence.

1. Karl was _____ that the store was closed; he really wanted a bag of chips.

    a. intimate   b. irate   c. intimidated   d. inaccurate

2. Laurene _____ her free time to helping children learn to read.

    a. establishes   b. laments   c. devotes   d. beguiles

3. Dan showed his _____ when he bought low and sold high in the stock market.

    a. sympathy   b. shrewdness   c. claim   d. inspection

4. Lizzy _____ ever taking the trip; it was one disaster after another.

    a. kindled   b. lamented   c. contradicted   d. neglected

5. I was shocked when Sumiko _____ her secret that she was from outer space.

    a. supervised   b. compromised   c. disclosed   d. wavered

6. I gave myself _____ time to drive to my grandmother's house, but I was still late because of a huge accident on the freeway that delayed me for three hours.

    a. ample   b. confidential   c. lavish   d. malicious

7. I took the time to _____ on how much I was studying and decided that I need to put more time into my school work if I want to learn anything.

    a. waver   b. affront   c. immerse   d. reflect

8. Katy worked hard to _____ front row seats at the tennis tournament; they were not easy to get.

    a. relate   b. secure   c. kindle   d. clarify

9. My professor thought my responses on the quiz were _____; she said I needed more details.

    a. vague   b. jubilant   c. passionate   d. weary

10. Sam's _____ was questioned when bags of the company's office supplies were found in the trunk of his car.

    a. bliss   b. harbinger   c. aside   d. integrity

© 2007 Pearson Education, Inc.

2 Finish the story using the vocabulary words below. Use each word once.

VOCABULARY LIST

affronted	apparently	assumed	circumstance	ensure
inaccurate	invincible	malicious	resolved	tumult

THE PARTY

I thought that throwing a party to show my appreciation to all my friends for their support when I was ill would be easy: I was wrong. My preliminary estimate that it would cost about $100 was way too low. I spent $105 on decorations, plates, and games alone. I then (1)_____ to make a firm budget. To (2)_____ a successful party, I would need to plan carefully.

After the (3)_____ of getting ready for the party, I admired how nice my house looked. I was encouraged about the success of the party when the first guests complimented me on the good food and beautiful decorations. Then something remarkable happened, and the mood of the party began to change as more people came. My awareness of the problem was slow, but I came to feel that there was tension in the room. I couldn't figure out what (4)_____ was causing people to start whispering in small groups. To verify that something was going on, I asked my best friend for her opinion. She told me that someone had started a (5)_____ story about me. I was (6)_____ that someone would say mean things about me. How could one of my friends do that? I cautiously tried to find the identity of the person who was spreading the gossip. His or her cover, however, was (7)_____.

Finally, I stood up on a chair and said, "For the benefit of everyone here, I want to announce that the story circulating about me is (8)_____. Someone has made a huge mistake about my illness. The support of real friends has empowered me to make this statement. I had (9)_____ that everyone here was a friend. (10)_____, I was wrong. To those people who really do care about me, thank you for coming to my party." As the clapping began, I heard the front door open and shut. I never figured out who left, but I enjoyed the rest of the evening with some great friends.

▊ ▊▊ ▊ INTERACTIVE EXERCISE

Answer the following questions to further test your understanding of the vocabulary words.

1. Whom would you share an intimate secret with? Why? _____

_____

2. When were you able to empathize with a friend? _____

_____

3. What is one of the most offensive smells to you? _____

_____

4. When were you willing to compromise? _____

_____

5. What are two events that it would be good to establish deadlines for?

_____   _____

6. What can someone do to become less gullible? _____

_____

7. What are two areas that are still uncharted in this world?

_____   _____

8. What topic do you have a genuine interest in? _____

_____

9. How many hours of sleep do you consider adequate for you? _____

_____

10. In what type of situation would someone try to be congenial? _____

_____

© 2007 Pearson Education, Inc.

CROSSWORD PUZZLE

Use the following words to complete the crossword puzzle. Use each word once.

VOCABULARY LIST

advice	aspect	beguile	claim	clarify
disclose	genesis	harbinger	impress	inevitable
interim	juncture	lavish	manipulative	naive
neglect	query	relate	sympathy	vital

Across

1. beginning
7. this can be good or bad
8. essential, such as breathing
11. to interest or influence
13. certain
14. swimsuit sales: means summer's near
16. a moment
18. simple or innocent
19. a part or an expression
20. temporary

Down

2. card one would send a recent widow
3. extravagant
4. to make public
5. to charm
6. controlling
9. to ask
10. a declaration or assertion
12. to tell or report
15. to overlook
17. to make clear

© 2007 Pearson Education, Inc.

HINT

A World of Words

Keep your eyes open for new words. You will certainly encounter new words in the textbooks you read in college and in the lectures your professors give, but new words can be found everywhere. Don't turn off your learning when you leave the classroom. When you see a new word in the newspaper or on a poster downtown or even on a fortune cookie, use the strategies you have learned in this book: look for context clues around the new word, try to predict the meaning, and check the dictionary if you aren't sure of the meaning. No matter where you are or what age you may be, your vocabulary can continue to grow.

▌▌▐▌▌ COLLABORATIVE ACTIVITY: DRAMA

Charades: You may be given one of the following words to act out in class, or you may want to do this activity with a study group. Think about how these words can be demonstrated without speaking. The other people will try to guess what word you are showing.

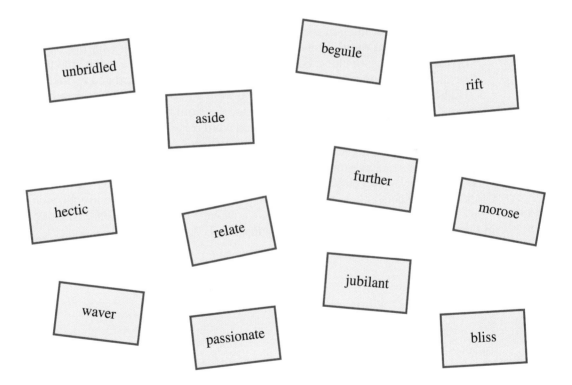

CREATE YOUR OWN FLASH CARDS

Using flash cards can be an immensely helpful way to study vocabulary words. The process of making the flash cards will aid you in remembering the meanings of the words. Index cards work well as flash cards. Put the word and the pronunciation on the front of the card. Elements you may want to include on the back of the cards will vary according to the word and your preferred learning style. Consider the ideas below and find what works best for you.

1. **The part of speech**: Write an abbreviation for the part of speech, such as n. for noun or v. for verb. This addition will help when you are writing sentences.
2. **A simple definition**: Use the definitions in the book or modify them to something that has meaning for you. Use a definition you can remember.
3. **A sentence**: Make up your own sentence that correctly uses the word. Try to use a context clue to help you remember the word. It might help to put yourself or friends in the sentences to personalize your use of the word. If you really like a sentence from the book, you can use that too.
4. **A drawing**: If you are a visual learner, try drawing the word. Some words especially lend themselves to this method. Your drawing doesn't have to be fancy; it should just help you remember the meaning of the word.
5. **A mnemonic (ni mon' ik) device**: These are methods to help your memory. They can be rhymes, formulas, or clues. For example: Stationery with an *e* is the kind that goes in an *e*nvelope. Make up any connections you can between the word and its meaning.
6. **Highlight word parts**: Circle one or more word parts (prefixes, roots, or suffixes) that appear in the word and write the meaning(s) next to the word part: for example, ⟨dis⟩organized. See the Word Parts chapters in the text for more on word parts.　　　　　⟶ *not*

Whatever you do, make the cards personally meaningful. Find the techniques that work for you and use them in creating your cards. Then make the time to study the cards. Carry them with you and study any chance you get. Also, find someone who will be tough in quizzing you with the cards. Have the person hold up a card, and you give the meaning and use the word in a sentence. Don't quit until you are confident that you know what each word means. You may use the following pages of flash card templates to get you started.

Sample card

Front　　　　　　　　　　　　　　　　　　　　　　　　Back

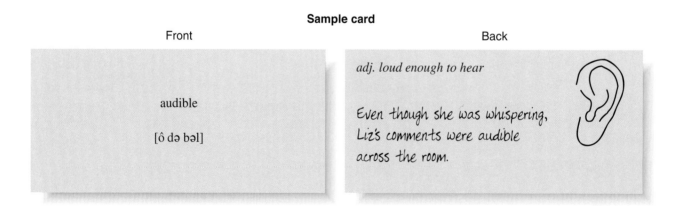

audible

[ô də bəl]

adj. loud enough to hear

Even though she was whispering, Liz's comments were audible across the room.

FLASH CARDS

WORD LIST